of prayer with

SAINT FAUSTINA KOWALSKA

C000066551

15 days
of prayer series

On a journey, it's good to have a guide. Even great saints took spiritual directors or confessors with them on their itineraries toward sanctity. Now you can be guided by the most influential spiritual figures of all time. The 15 Days of Prayer series introduces their deepest and most personal thoughts.

This popular series is perfect if you are looking for a gift, or if you want to be introduced to a particular guide and his or her spirituality. Each volume contains:

- ⌘ A brief biography of the saint or spiritual leader
- ⌘ A guide to creating a format for prayer or retreat
- ⌘ Fifteen meditation sessions with focus points and reflection guides

15 days
of prayer with
SAINT FAUSTINA KOWALSKA

JOHN J. CLEARY

NEW CITY PRESS
Hyde Park, NY

Published in the United States by New City Press
202 Comforter Blvd., Hyde Park, NY 12538
www.newcitypress.com
©2010 John J. Cleary (compilation)

Diary, St. Maria Faustina Kowalska
©1987 Congregation of Marians
of the Immaculate Conception
Stockbridge, MA 01263.
All rights reserved. Used with permission.

Cover design by Durva Correia

Scripture quotations are taken from the *New Revised Standard Version Bible*,
copyright 1989 by the Division of Christian Education of the National
Council of the Churches of Christ in the U.S.A. Used by permission. All
rights reserved.

Printed in the United States of America

Contents

How to Use This Book

An old Chinese proverb, or at least what I am able to recall of what is supposed to be an old Chinese proverb, goes something like this: "Even a journey of a thousand miles begins with a single step." When you think about it, the truth of the proverb is obvious. It is impossible to begin any project, let alone a journey, without taking the first step. I think it might also be true, although I cannot recall if another Chinese proverb says it, "that the first step is often the hardest." Or, as someone else once observed, "the distance between a thought and the corresponding action needed to implement the idea takes the most energy." I don't know who shared that perception with me but I am certain it was not an old Chinese master!

With this ancient proverbial wisdom, and the not-so-ancient wisdom of an unknown contemporary sage still fresh, we move from proverbs to presumptions. How do these relate to the task before us?

I am presuming that if you are reading this introduction it is because you are contemplating a journey. My presumption is that you are preparing for a spiritual journey and that you have taken at least some of the first steps necessary to prepare for this journey. I also presume, and please excuse me if I am making too many presumptions, that in your preparation for the spiritual journey you have determined that you need a guide. From deep within the recesses of your deepest self, there was something that called you to consider Saint Faustina as a potential companion. If my presumptions are correct, may I congratulate you on this decision? I think you have made a wise choice, a choice that can be confirmed by yet another source of wisdom, the wisdom that comes from practical experience.

Even an informal poll of experienced travelers will reveal a common opinion; it is very difficult to travel alone. Some might observe that it is even foolish. Still others may be even stronger in their opinion and go so far as to insist that it is necessary to have a guide, especially when you are traveling into uncharted waters and into territory that you have not yet experienced. I am of the personal opinion that a traveling companion is welcome under all circumstances. The thought of traveling alone, to some exciting destination without someone to share the journey with does not capture my imagination or channel my enthusiasm. However, with that being noted, what is simply a matter of preference on the normal journey becomes a matter of necessity when a person embarks on a spiritual journey.

The spiritual journey, which can be the most challenging of all journeys, is experienced best with a guide, a companion, or at the very least, a friend in whom you have placed your trust. This observation is not a preference or an opinion but rather an established spiritual necessity. All of the great saints with whom I am familiar had a spiritual director or a confessor who journeyed with them. Admittedly, at times the saint might well have traveled far beyond the experience of their guide and companion but more often than not they would return to their director and reflect on their experience. Understood in this sense, the director and companion provided a valuable contribution and necessary resource. When I was learning how to pray (a necessity for anyone who desires to be a full-time and public "religious person"), the community of men that I belong to gave me a great gift. Between my second and third year in college, I was given a one-year sabbatical, with all expenses paid and all of my personal needs met. This period of time was called novitiate. I was officially designated as a novice, a beginner in the spiritual journey, and I was

assigned a "master," a person who was willing to lead me. In addition to the master, I was
provided with every imaginable book and any
other resource that I could possibly need. Even
with all that I was provided, I did not learn how
to pray because of the books and the unlimited
resources, rather it was the master, the companion who was the key to the experience.

One day, after about three months of reading,
of quiet and solitude, and of practicing all of the
methods and descriptions of prayer that were
available to me, the master called. "Put away
the books, forget the method, and just listen."
We went into a room, became quiet, and tried to
recall the presence of God, and then, the master
simply prayed out loud and permitted me to listen to his prayer. As he prayed, he revealed his
hopes, his dreams, his struggles, his successes,
and most of all, his relationship with God. I discovered as I listened that his prayer was deeply
intimate but most of all it was self-revealing. As
I learned about him, I was led through his life
experience to the place where God dwells. At
that moment I was able to understand a little
bit about what I was supposed to do if I really
wanted to pray.

The dynamic of what happened when the
master called, invited me to listen, and then
revealed his innermost self to me as he com-
municated with God in prayer, was important.

It wasn't so much that the master was trying to reveal to me what needed to be said; he was not inviting me to pray with the same words that he used, but rather that he was trying to bring me to that place within myself where prayer becomes possible. That place, a place of intimacy and of self-awareness, was a necessary stop on the journey and it was a place that I needed to be led to. I could not have easily discovered it on my own.

The purpose of the volume that you hold in your hand is to lead you, over a period of fifteen days or, maybe more realistically, fifteen prayer periods, to a place where prayer is possible. If you already have a regular experience and practice of prayer, perhaps this volume can help lead you to a deeper place, a more intimate relationship with the Lord.

It is important to note that the purpose of this book is not to lead you to a better relationship with Saint Faustina, your spiritual companion. Although your companion will invite you to share some of her deepest and most intimate thoughts, your companion is doing so only to bring you to that place where God dwells. After all, the true measurement of all companions for the journey is that they bring you to the place where you need to be, and then they step back, out of the picture. A guide who brings you to the desired destination and then sticks around is a very unwelcome guest!

Many times I have found myself attracted to a particular idea or method for accomplishing a task, only to discover that what seemed to be inviting and helpful possessed too many details. All of my energy went to the mastery of the details and I soon lost my enthusiasm. In each instance, the book that seemed so promising ended up on my bookshelf, gathering dust. I can assure you, it is not our intention that this book end up in your bookcase, filled with promise, but unable to deliver.

There are three simple rules that need to be followed in order to use this book with a measure of satisfaction.

Place: It is important that you choose a place for reading that provides the necessary atmosphere for reflection and that does not allow for too many distractions. Whatever place you choose needs to be comfortable, have the necessary lighting, and, finally, have a sense of "welcoming" about it. You need to be able to look forward to the experience of the journey. Don't travel steerage if you know you will be more comfortable in first class and if the choice is realistic for you. On the other hand, if first class is a distraction and you feel more comfortable and more yourself in steerage, then it is in steerage that you belong.

My favorite place is an overstuffed and comfortable chair in my bedroom. There is a light over my shoulder, and the chair reclines if I feel a need to recline. Once in a while, I get lucky and the sun comes through my window and bathes the entire room in light. I have other options and other places that are available to me but this is the place that I prefer.

Time: Choose a time during the day when you are most alert and when you are most receptive to reflection, meditation, and prayer. The time that you choose is an essential component. If you are a morning person, for example, you should choose a time that is in the morning. If you are more alert in the afternoon, choose an afternoon time slot; and if evening is your preference, then by all means choose the evening. Try to avoid "peak" periods in your daily routine when you know that you might be disturbed. The time that you choose needs to be your time and needs to work for you.

It is also important that you choose how much time you will spend with your companion each day. For some it will be possible to set aside enough time in order to read and reflect on all the material that is offered for a given day. For others, it might not be possible to devote one time to the suggested material for the day, so the prayer period may need to be extended for two, three, or even more sessions. It is not important how long it takes you; it is only important that it works for you and that you remain committed to that which is possible.

For myself I have found that fifteen minutes in the early morning, while I am still in my robe and pajamas and before my morning coffee, and even before I prepare myself for the day, is the best time. No one expects to see me or to interact with me because I have not yet "announced" the fact that I am awake or even on the move. However, once someone hears me in the bathroom, then my window of opportunity is gone. It is therefore important to me that I use the time that I have identified when it is available to me.

Freedom: It may seem strange to suggest that freedom is the third necessary ingredient, but I have discovered that it is most important. By freedom I understand a certain "stance toward life," a "permission to be myself and to be gentle and understanding of who I am." I am constantly amazed at how the human person so easily sets himself or herself up for disappointment and perceived failure. We so easily make judgments about ourselves and our actions and our choices, and very often those judgments are negative, and not at all helpful.

For instance, what does it really matter if I have chosen a place and a time, and I have missed both the place and the time for three days in a row? What does it matter if I have chosen, in that twilight time before I am completely awake and still a little sleepy, to roll over and to sleep for fifteen minutes more? Does it mean that I am not serious about the journey, that I really don't want to pray, that I am just fooling myself when I say that my prayer time is important to me? Perhaps, but I prefer to believe that it simply means that I am tired and I just wanted a little more sleep. It doesn't mean anything more than that. However, if I make it mean more than that, then I can become discouraged, frustrated, and put myself into a state where I might more easily give up. "What's the use? I might as well forget all about it."

The same sense of freedom applies to the reading and the praying of this text. If I do not find the introduction to each day helpful, I don't need to read it. If I find the questions for reflection at the end of the appointed day repetitive, then I should choose to close the book and go my own way. Even if I discover that the reflection offered for the day is not the one that I prefer and that the one for the next day seems more inviting, then by all means, go on to the one for the next day.

That's it! If you apply these simple rules to your journey you should receive the maximum benefit and you will soon find yourself at your destination. But be prepared to be surprised. If you have never been on a spiritual journey you should know that the "travel brochures" and the other descriptions that you might have heard are nothing compared to the real thing. There is so much more than you can imagine.

A final prayer of blessing suggests itself:

Lord, catch me off guard today.
Surprise me with some moment of
        beauty or pain
So that at least for the moment
I may be startled into seeing that you
    are here in all your splendor,
Always and everywhere,
Barely hidden,
Beneath,
Beyond,
Within this life I breathe.

Frederick Buechner

Rev. Thomas M. Santa, CSsR
Liguori, Missouri

A Brief Chronology of Saint Faustina Kowalska's Life

August 25, 1905:

Helen Kowalska is born in the village of Glogowiec, Turek County, Lodz Province, Poland.

August 27, 1905:

Helen is baptized in St. Casimir Church.

1912: For the first time in her life, seven-year-old Helen hears a voice in her soul, calling her to a more perfect way of life.

1922: Helen tells her parents that she would like to join a convent. Her parents are against this decision.

1922–1923:

Helen works as a house servant for several families.

1924: Helen enters a convent in Warsaw. She applies at the Congregation of the Sisters of Our Lady of Mercy. Seeking to determine the extent of her commitment to a religious vocation, the superior tests Helen, telling her to go to work so she can pay for her wardrobe.

August 1, 1925:

Helen again applies to the Congregation of the Sisters of Our Lady of Mercy. This time she is accepted.

April 30, 1926:

After an eight-day retreat, Helen receives her habit and her name as a religious, Sister Maria Faustina.

April 3, 1927:

Sister Faustina experiences a spiritual "dark night." This trial spans nearly her entire period as a novice.

April 16, 1928:

On Good Friday, the fire of Divine Love envelops the suffering novice. Sister Faustina forgets her past hardships, and recognizes more clearly how much Christ suffered for her.

April 30, 1928:

Sister Faustina makes her first profession of temporary vows. She renews these vows each year for the next five years, when she makes her perpetual vows.

February 22, 1931:

Jesus appears to Sister Faustina in a vision; he tells her to produce a painting according to the image she sees.

June 1934:

The painting of the Divine Mercy image, by artist E. Kazimierowski, under the guidance of Sister Faustina, is completed. Sister Faustina cries because the image of the Lord Jesus in the painting is not as beautiful as the vision she had earlier beheld.

July 28, 1934:

Sister Faustina resumes writing her diary of mystical experiences and innermost thoughts in obedience to her spiritual director and Jesus Christ.

January 8, 1936:

Sister Faustina visits Bishop Jalbrzykowski and declares that the Lord is demanding the founding of a new congregation.

December 9, 1936:

Due to her declining health, Sister Faustina is sent to the hospital in Pradnik, a sanatorium for tuberculosis patients in Cracow.

June 1938:

> Sister Faustina stops writing her diary.

October 5, 1938:

> After suffering greatly with so much patience, Sister Maria Faustina dies.

October 21, 1965:

> The Informative Process relating to the life and virtues of Sister Faustina commences. From this moment, Sister Faustina is worthy of the title, Servant of God.

January 31, 1968:

> The process of the beatification of Sister Faustina H. Kowalska is formally inaugurated.

April 18, 1993:

> Sister Faustina is beatified by Pope John Paul II in St. Peter's Square in Vatican City.

April 30, 2000:

> Sister Faustina Kowalska is canonized by Pope John Paul II. In his canonization homily, the pope announces that the Second Sunday of Easter will be known as Divine Mercy Sunday.

May 5, 2000:

> By Vatican decree the Second Sunday of Easter is established as Divine Mercy Sunday for the universal Church.

Introduction

Read the words of a contemporary Jewish mystic: "It is easier for us to believe in the wrath of God than in his mercy, for wrath is a feeling that is very human, while mercy is divine." However unfair and foolish it might be, there is a tendency — all too human, of course — to understand the qualities of God as we have come to know our own human qualities in our own human experience. It is not so much that we think less of God; but we do have a tendency at times to think of ourselves and how we react to a given situation when we attempt to understand how the Divine might feel.

We can be petty at times. We can be cruel. How many examples of hard-hearted and wrathful judgments can we select from our collective and individual memories? These hard-hearted judgments we hold toward others and those hard-hearted judgments that others hold toward ourselves most likely number far more than those times in our lives when we have known true mercy and tender forgiveness. We believe in the wrath of God because we've felt wrath so deeply in our experience with each other. We

personify God accordingly, rarely pausing to
contemplate the Divine Mercy that saturates the
pages of our Bibles.

A Christian mystic who lived during the first
half of the twentieth century was well aware of
the total and complete mercy offered to us by the
Divine. Saint Faustina Kowalska is the Apostle
of Divine Mercy and Secretary of the Lord; hers
is the loud, sure voice proclaiming the mercy of
God so often forgotten, so frequently swept to
the shadows as so many people choose to focus
on the judgment and wrath of a God who wants
nothing more than to love and be loved by the
men and women he has created in love.

This book, *Fifteen Days of Prayer with Saint
Faustina Kowalska*, is written with the hope that
it will help to facilitate an experience of God's
great mercy for all his people and specifically for
you, the reader. These fifteen days of personal
retreat will focus directly on the life and the
words of Saint Faustina. Her life is a journey of
trust in Jesus Christ, of knowing the healing and
comfort his great mercy provides.

In 1935, Sister Faustina experienced a vision
in which the Lord revealed a wonderful and powerful prayer, a prayer he desires everyone to say
— the Chaplet of Divine Mercy. The Lord promised Faustina that anyone who recites the chaplet
will be given extraordinary graces. The Chaplet
of Divine Mercy will be the prayer that centers
our oft-confused heart on the peace and goodness
of God. Each day of this retreat will close with a
recitation of the Chaplet of Divine Mercy — the

prayer Jesus gave us through Faustina. A guide as to how to recite the Chaplet of Divine Mercy on ordinary rosary beads is provided on page 27.

Trusting wholly in the Lord and proclaiming the mercy of God for his people — this was the mission of Saint Faustina Kowalska. Through this saint we are given a prayer, the Chaplet of Divine Mercy, so that we might come to trust the Lord with our entire being, and experience the grace and goodness of his mercy. Trust and mercy are at the center of this book. We have all come to know wrath in our lives; we have all felt the pain it brings. Let us now come to trust in the mercy our Lord Jesus Christ desires us to know. Saint Faustina is our willing guide, joyously waiting to take each of us by the hand, ready to continue her service to Jesus when he first called out to her:

> My daughter, tell the whole world about my mercy and my love. The flames of mercy are burning within me. I desire to pour them out upon human souls. Oh, what pain they cause me when they do not want to accept them! Tell aching mankind to snuggle close to my merciful heart and I will fill it with peace. Tell all people that I am Love and Mercy itself. When a soul approaches me with trust, I fill it with such an abundance of graces it cannot contain them within itself, but radiates them to other souls (Diary 1074).

A Few Notes
About Saint Faustina
Kowalska

The Apostle of Mercy

Saint Maria Faustina was born Helenka Kowalska in the village of Glogowiec, west of Lodz, Poland, on August 25, 1905. She was the third of ten children. When she was nearly twenty years old, she entered the Congregation of the Sisters of Our Lady of Mercy, whose members devote themselves to the care and education of troubled young women. The following year she received her religious habit and was given the name Sister Maria Faustina, to which she added "of the Most Blessed Sacrament," as was permitted by her Congregation's custom. In the 1930s Saint Faustina received from the Lord a message of mercy that she was told to spread throughout the world. She was asked to become the apostle and secretary of God's mercy, a model of how to be merciful to others, and an instrument for reemphasizing God's plan of mercy for the whole world. It was not a glamorous prospect. Her entire life, in imitation of Christ's, was to be a sacrifice — a life lived for others. At the Divine Lord's request, she willingly offered her personal sufferings in union with him to atone for the sins of others; in her daily life, she was to become a doer of mercy by bringing joy and peace to others. By writing about God's mercy she was to encourage others to trust in him and thus prepare the whole world for his second coming.

Convinced of her own unworthiness and terrified at the thought of trying to write anything, she nonetheless began keeping a diary in obedience to the express wishes of Jesus as well as her spiritual director. For four years she recorded divine revelations and mystical experiences, together with her own innermost thoughts, insights, and prayers. The result is a book of some six hundred pages that, in simple language, repeats and clarifies the gospel story of God's love for his people. Among the many reflections, the diary stresses above all else the need to trust God implicitly.

Saint Faustina's spiritual life was based on deep humility, purity of intention, and loving obedience to God in imitation of the virtues of the Blessed Virgin Mary. Her special devotion to Mary Immaculate and to the sacraments of the

Eucharist and penance gave her the strength to bear all her sufferings as an offering to God on behalf of the Church and those in special need, especially great sinners and the dying. She actually wrote and suffered in secret, with only her spiritual director and some of the superiors aware that anything special was taking place in her life. After her death from tuberculosis on October 5, 1938, even her closest associates were amazed as they began to discover what great sufferings and deep mystical experiences had been given to this sister of theirs, who had always been so cheerful and humble. She had taken deeply into her heart God's gospel command to "be merciful, just as your Father is merciful" (Lk 6:36). Her confessor similarly encouraged Sister Faustina to act in such a way that everyone who came in contact with her would go away joyful.

The message of mercy that Saint Faustina received has been spread all over the world. She has been recognized as a true mystic and her diary — entitled "Divine Mercy in My Soul" — has become the principle resource for devotion to the Divine Mercy. Jesus revealed to her that the message of his mercy would spread precisely through her writings for the great benefit of souls.

On Mercy Sunday, April 30, 2000, Pope John Paul II raised Saint Faustina to the altar of sanctity.

How to Recite the Chaplet of Divine Mercy

*P*rayed on ordinary rosary beads, the chaplet is an intercessory prayer that extends the offering of the holy Eucharist. It may be said at any time, but our Lord expressly requested that it be used as a novena on the nine days preceding the feast of Divine Mercy (the first Sunday after Easter).

It is also particularly appropriate to say the chaplet during the three o'clock hour (bringing to mind the time of Christ's death on the cross). In his revelations to Saint Faustina, Jesus asked for special prayer and veneration for his passion during this time.

1. The Sign of the Cross

In the name of the Father, and of the Son, and of the Holy Spirit. Amen

2. Opening Prayers (optional)

You expired, Jesus, but the source of life gushed forth for souls, and the ocean of mercy opened up for the whole world. O Fount of Life, unfathomable Divine Mercy, envelop the whole world and empty Yourself out upon us (Diary 1319).

O Blood and Water, which gushed forth from the Heart of Jesus as a fount of mercy for us, I trust in You! (Three times) (Diary 84).

3. The Our Father

Our Father, who art in heaven, hallowed be thy name. Thy kingdom come; thy will be done on earth as it is in heaven. Give us this day our daily bread; and forgive us our trespasses as we forgive those who trespass against us; and lead us not into temptation, but deliver us from evil. Amen.

4. The Hail Mary

Hail Mary, full of grace! The Lord is with you. Blessed are you among women, and blessed is the fruit of your womb, Jesus. Holy Mary, Mother of God, pray for us sinners, now and at the hour of our death. Amen.

5. The Apostles' Creed

I believe in God, the Father almighty, creator of heaven and earth.

I believe in Jesus Christ, his only Son, our Lord. He was conceived by the power of the Holy Spirit, and born of the Virgin Mary. He suffered under Pontius Pilate, was crucified, died, and was buried. He descended into hell. On the third day he rose again. He ascended into heaven, and is seated at the right hand of the Father. He will come again to judge the living and the dead.

I believe in the Holy Spirit, the holy Catholic Church, the communion of saints, the forgiveness of sins, the resurrection of the body, and life everlasting. Amen.

6. On the "Our Father" Bead Before Each Decade:

Eternal Father, I offer You the Body and Blood, Soul and Divinity of Your dearly beloved Son, Our Lord Jesus Christ, in atonement for our sins and those of the whole world (Diary 476).

7. On the "Hail Mary" Beads of Each Decade:

For the sake of His sorrowful Passion, have mercy on us and on the whole world.

8. After Five Decades, the Concluding Doxology (Three Times):

Holy God, Holy Mighty One, Holy Immortal One, have mercy on us and on the whole world.

9. Closing Prayer (Optional):

Eternal God, in whom mercy is endless, and the treasury of compassion inexhaustible, look kindly upon us, and increase Your mercy in us, that in difficult moments we might not despair, nor become despondent, but with great confidence submit ourselves to Your holy will, which is Love and Mercy itself. Amen (Diary 950).

1
The Lord Is Calling

Focus Point

////////////

From the outset of her life, Faustina Kowalska was called by Jesus to a very special life. And though coming to answer this call developed slowly and with difficulty, Faustina persevered through the obstacles she encountered, remaining true to God's will that his servant serve in the capacity of the religious life. Faustina's life was beset by numerous struggles even after she arrived at the convent, but her commitment to the Lord in her younger days would serve as the foundation to a life of devotion and service.

////////////

And so You see, Jesus, that everything is now up to You. I am perfectly at peace, despite these great urgings. (…) Your cause will be made apparent. I am totally in accord with Your will; do with me as You please, O Lord, but only grant me the grace of

loving You more and more ardently. This is what is
most precious to me. I desire nothing but You, O Love
Eternal! It matters not along what paths You will lead
me, paths of pain or paths of joy. I want to love You
at every moment of my life. If You tell me to leave, O
Jesus, in order to carry out Your will, I will leave. If
You tell me to stay, I will stay. It matters not what I
suffer, in the one instance or the other (Diary 751).

////////////

*B*orn in the geographical center of Poland on
August 25, 1905, Helen Kowalska was the
third of ten children born to carpenter/farmer
Stanislaus Kowalski and his wife, Marianna.
To her mother, she was Helenka (her baptized
name was "Helena"); but to the rest of the world
she would become known as Saint Faustina
Kowalska, Secretary of the Lord and Apostle
of Divine Mercy. Her life was a continuous
endeavor to abandon her own will for that of
the Lord's. During her brief life, Faustina would
come to experience great mystical insights, dark
spiritual "nights," and great trust in the mercy of
Jesus Christ. This was a woman of deep commitment and unflinching faith. She is a model
for our time, a model for all time.

Helen's younger days were spent on the family farm, far from the noise and political unrest
of the larger Polish cities. It was on this farm
that Helen learned her prayers at a very early

age. A strong faith was instilled in Helen during these years: this faith was due in no small part to a strict and religiously-demanding father who never missed a Sunday Mass, and a mother whose service to her family was a deep reminder of God's abiding love for his children. Helen would often spend long periods alone in prayer, deep into the night. Where most children are restless in the midst of quiet stillness, Helen cherished these moments with God, recognizing the presence of the Lord surrounding her, and she waited on his words.

When she was just seven years old, Helen heard the call for the first time. It was during the exposition of the Blessed Sacrament, during vespers, that she heard God's voice calling her to a deeper, more perfect way of life. At the time, Helen did not know what to make of this call. Only later in life, looking back on that moment, did Helen realize she was being called to the religious life.

Helen grew in holiness throughout her childhood, receiving the sacraments of penance and Holy Communion. Like her father, she was committed to never missing a Sunday Mass, even if it meant seeing to all her chores very early in the morning, before anyone else in the family had even stirred in their beds! Helen's goodness and love for God blossomed, and all who encountered her were moved by her spirit and good will.

Due to the ravages of World War I, Poland was victim to poverty and destruction, and Helen's family was not spared the consequences. The Kowalski family struggled to make ends meet during this period, and the children's tattered clothing had to suffice for need of food. It was at this time that Helen received the little formal education she would come to have (about two years) before she was told by the authorities that the education of younger children took precedence over her own. By this time (1919), Helen was fourteen years old. Strange and wonderful things were soon to come.

For the next two years, Helen was at work in her family home, quietly attending to her duties of cleaning and cooking. Her spiritual life intensified during this time — especially at night, when she would see odd, bright lights during her prayer sessions. God's call was becoming clearer to the sixteen-year-old, and though she could not yet identify specifically the path she was to pursue, she was aware that serving in the family home was no longer the life God asked of her.

In 1921, Helen's mother granted her daughter permission to work as a housemaid outside the family home. During her first year as a paid housemaid, Helen worked cheerfully and prayed constantly. It was during this time that she fully realized she was being called to a life in the convent as a religious sister. She would have to work as a housemaid for three more years to afford the dowry — the clothing and finances needed to enter the convent.

It was during this three-year period, at a dance she attended one evening with her sister Josephine, that Helen experienced a mystical vision in which a wounded and bloodied Jesus appeared to her, asking, "How long shall I put up with you and how long will you keep putting me off?" (Diary 9). Helen left the dance in a daze, and made her way to the Cathedral of St. Stanislas Kotska, where she fell into prayer. Prostrate before the Blessed Sacrament, Helen asked Jesus what he wanted of her. She heard these words in reply: "Go at once to Warsaw; you will enter a convent there."

Trusting everything to Jesus, Helen returned to her uncle's house, where she had been staying. She tried with great difficulty to explain to her sister everything that was going on inside of her. After asking her sister to say goodbye to her parents on her behalf, and taking with her only the dress she was wearing, Helen boarded a train for Warsaw. When she arrived in Warsaw, Helen prayed to the Blessed Virgin Mary for guidance. While she waited in a church during one of the Masses, Helen was told by a voice to consult with the celebrant of that Mass as to what she should do next. After speaking with the priest, Helen was sent to the home of a trusted and holy woman, Mrs. Aldona Lipszyc, where Helen would work as a housemaid until she made enough money to enter the convent.

During her one year of cheerful and loving service to Mrs. Lipszyc and her family, Helen sought out to find a convent that would accept her. This proved to be quite difficult. Convent after convent refused her — her limited education, poor appearance, and life as a housemaid surely playing a part in her rejections. Helen cried out to Jesus in her discouraged and saddened state, begging for his help. It was not long after this plea that Helen came to the door of the convent of the Sisters of Our Lady of Mercy and met with the Mother Superior there.

Mother General Michael met with Helen and saw there was much to like about the cheerful young woman with the warm smile. She *was* uneducated and her lack of funds *was* an issue, but Mother Michael did see a genuine calling at work in Helen. So she asked Helen to go into the convent chapel and ask the Lord what he had to say on the matter of Helen entering the convent:

> With great joy, I went to the chapel and asked Jesus: "Lord of this house, do You accept me? This is how one of the sisters told me to put the question to You." Immediately I heard this voice: "I do accept; you are in My Heart." When I returned from the chapel, Mother

> Superior asked first of all, "Well, has the Lord accepted you?" I answered, "Yes." "If the Lord has accepted, [she said] then I also will accept" (Diary 14).

Helen continued to work for Mrs. Lipszyc until she had earned enough money to afford the wardrobe necessary to join the convent. Jesus was on her mind constantly during this period, and Helen would often sing the hymn "The Hidden Jesus" ("Jezusa Ukrytego") to inspire and comfort herself as she prepared to enter the convent:

> Jesus hidden in the Blessed Sacrament,
> Him I must adore;
> Renounce everything for His sake,
> Live only by His love.

Helen Kowalska officially entered the convent of the Sisters of Our Lady of Mercy on August 1, 1925. The young woman who had followed the call of God through the doorway of a convent was overwhelmed with joy, thankful to her Lord for the graces that had made her happiness possible.

Let us now pray the Chaplet of Divine Mercy (page 27)....

Reflection Questions

Do I hear God calling me in my life to a special way of service as Faustina did? How do I
prepare myself to listen to his call? Do I make
time for God during my day? Do I prepare a
"space of silence" in my daily life during which
the Lord may speak to me and I may listen to his
will for my life? If I have heard his call and am
reluctant to act on it, what are those obstacles
that prevent me from doing so? Might I pray for
the grace of God to overcome these fears and
other obstacles that seem to be so daunting?

2

A Period of Darkness

Focus Point

////////////

Like many of the great saints throughout history, Faustina Kowalska suffered her own "Dark Night" of spiritual dryness, and persevered through the emotional and physical trials wrought by this period in her life. She didn't know why she was suffering so much, but her trust in God did not falter. Deep in her soul, Faustina knew God's will was at work, deepening the intensity of her dependence on God alone, and increasing her humility in the face of pain, rumor, and persecution. She suffered throughout her postulancy and novitiate, arriving at a state of joy and awe when she professed her perpetual vows to Jesus Christ.

////////////

A noble and delicate soul, even the most simple, but one of delicate sensibilities, sees God in everything, finds Him everywhere, and knows how to find Him in even the most hidden things, it thanks God for all things, it draws profit for the soul from all things, and it gives glory to God. It places its trust in God and is not confused when the time of ordeal comes. It knows that God is always the best of Fathers and makes little of human opinion. It follows faithfully the faintest breath of the Holy Spirit; it rejoices in this Spiritual Guest and holds onto Him like a child to its mother. Where other souls come to a standstill and fear, this soul passes on without fear or difficulty (Diary 148).

///////////////

*T*o find God in all things — this is a great challenge in life. When we stare at a sunset or look at a small child in his mother's arms, we easily feel the presence of God. It is right there in front of us. But what of the darker corners of our lives? What of those areas of suffering, cruelty, dryness, hatred, and desperation? Can we find God so readily there? Surely he is not present there. Ah, but he is! That is the truth of the matter. God is present, all around us. He never abandons his people. It might seem to us that God is not with us in a certain situation, and we feel alone, frightened, or angry. But it is at that very moment that we must become more aware and awaken to the reality of God all around us. Many of the great saints experienced precisely this "darkness," and Faustina Kowalska was no exception.

In late 1925, Helen was living as a postulant with the Sisters of Our Lady of Mercy, a congregation devoted to the rehabilitation of wayward women and girls, devoted to Mary, mother of Mercy, and devoted to the Mercy of God. Helen served in the convent kitchen during this time, expending great energy working and praying in her new environment. As a result of this exertion, Helen weakened and her health became a concern. The exhausted postulant was sent to the sisters' summer home in Skolimow for a period of rest.

While Helen was recuperating at her place of retreat, she did light work preparing meals for the two other sisters staying with her. But Helen was moved to pray, and she wanted to pray for the spiritual benefit of others, though she did not know specifically for whom to pray. As she conveys through her diary, she took her concerns to the Lord in prayer:

> Jesus said that on the following night He would let me know for whom I should pray.
>
> [The next night] I saw my Guardian Angel, who ordered me to follow him. In a moment I was in a misty place full of fire in which there was a great crowd of suffering souls. They were praying fervently, but to no avail, for themselves; only we can come to their

aid. The flames which were burning
them did not touch me at all…. I asked
these souls what their greatest suffering
was. They answered me in one voice
that their greatest torment was longing
for God. I saw Our Lady visiting the
souls in Purgatory. The souls call her
"The Star of the Sea." She brings them
refreshment…. We went out of that
prison of suffering. [I heard an interior
voice] which said, "My mercy does not
want this, but justice demands it." Since
that time, I am in closer communion
with the suffering souls (Diary 20).

This was Helen's first mystical vision of the
souls in purgatory.

On April 20, 1926, Helen received the habit
and veil as a novice of the Congregation of the
Sisters of Our Lady of Mercy. She was also
given a new name: Faustina (meaning happy
and blessed). Sister Maria Faustina would be a
novice for the next two years, studying religious
practices and conduct in convent life, and practicing the virtues. Formal study followed during
the second year.

Many of Faustina's fellow sisters greatly
enjoyed her presence among them. This pleas-
ant and humorous novice always had something
uplifting to say, and her dedication to humility
served as a model for others. There was no dis-

cernable ego in Faustina; everything she did or said was for Christ, to glorify his name. It mattered nothing to Faustina if she received credit from others for her loving service. With the grace of the Lord provided to her, Faustina worked in the convent kitchen with great enthusiasm and vigor.

As she approached the conclusion of her first year as a novice, Faustina began to experience a suffering in her soul, a "Dark Night." Faustina was without a spiritual director at this time, and was not aware that the trials she was experiencing had been common for saints throughout the ages as they journeyed along the path of growth in the Lord. Faustina was quite overwhelmed by the spiritual dryness she felt, and began praying a novena to Saint Thérèse of Lisieux, seeking the guidance of the "Little Flower." Thérèse appeared to her in a dream, and assured Faustina that despite the suffering she was enduring, God would "raise [her] to the altar as a saint" (see Diary 150).

With the date of profession of temporary vows fast approaching, Faustina was feeling quite anxious. Despite the kind words of Saint Thérèse, the spiritual dryness she experienced would not cease, and Faustina became exhausted both spiritually and physically. In this tortured state, Faustina threw herself into prayer. One night, she was visited by Mary, the Mother of God, who carried in her arms the Infant Jesus:

> My soul was filled with joy, and I said,
> "Mary, my Mother, do You know how
> terribly I suffer?" And the Mother of
> God answered me, "I know how much
> you suffer, but do not be afraid. I share
> with you your suffering, and I shall
> always do so." She smiled warmly and
> disappeared (Diary 25).

Faustina was comforted only briefly by these words, and her spiritual suffering began again the following day. Despite these sufferings, Faustina committed herself to silent suffering without complaint.

Even after her first profession of temporary vows (April 30, 1928), Faustina felt this spiritual dryness, and her yearning for God intensified. Then one night, during evening adoration:

> The Divine Presence invaded me, and
> I forgot everything else. Jesus gave me
> to understand how much He had suf-
> fered for me. This lasted a very short
> time. An intense yearning — a longing
> to love God (Diary 26).

It was revealed by the Lord to Faustina how much Jesus had suffered for all humanity and, in especially, Faustina herself. Faustina's spiritual dryness would persist for another six-month period, during which time she would experience little consolation and much physical weakness. Faustina felt very alone when she heard that some of her fellow sisters were spreading rumors that she was feigning illness or that she was possessed. No one around her understood the advanced spiritual ordeals she suffered, but the Lord provided Faustina visions of a future spiritual director — Fr. Michael Sopocko — who would help her understand God's will at a deeper level and accept the physical suffering, spiritual dryness, and persecution of others toward her in a spirit of humility and patience. These visions encouraged Faustina greatly, and her trust that the Lord would provide any and all graces for her benefit continued to grow.

Faustina made her perpetual vows on May 1, 1933, and was betrothed eternally to Jesus Christ. She recorded the power of the moment, her trust in God's will, and her reliance on his mercy in her diary:

> As the Bishop [Rospond] was putting the ring on my finger, God pervaded my whole being, and since I cannot express that moment, I will be silent about it. My relationship with God, since perpetual vows, has been more intimate than it had ever been before…. Thank You, Jesus, for the great favor of making known to me the whole abyss of my misery. I know that I am an abyss of nothingness and that, if Your holy grace

did not hold me up, I would return to nothingness in a moment. And so, with every beat of my heart, I thank You, my God, for Your great mercy towards me (Diary 254, 256).

Let us now pray the Chaplet of Divine Mercy (page 27)....

Reflection Questions

How do I respond to periods of spiritual dryness in my life? Do I persevere in prayer or am I so discouraged that I stop praying? Might I take comfort in the struggles and persistent faith and trust of Saint Faustina? If I am finding spiritual dryness to be a constant in my prayer life, might I consider meeting with a spiritual director to discuss what steps I might take in addressing this concern?

3
Divine Mercy Revealed

Focus Point

//////////////

In a vision, Jesus asked Sister Faustina to paint the Image of the Divine Mercy. Faustina complied, and an artist was hired to complete the task under her direction. Many versions of this image of Jesus — with two rays emanating from his chest — have been painted over the years and they are venerated in many churches all over the world. The Image of the Divine Mercy continues to serve as a conduit of grace to all those who revere it with trust and confidence in the mercy of God.

//////////////

Once, when I was visiting the artist who was painting the image, and saw that it was not as beautiful as Jesus is, I felt very sad about it, but I hid this deep in my heart. When we had left the artist's house, Mother Superior stayed in town to attend to some matters while I returned home alone. I went immediately to

*the chapel and wept a good deal. I said to the Lord,
"Who will paint You as beautiful as You are?" Then
I heard these words: "Not in the beauty of the color,
nor of the brush lies the greatness of this image, but
in My grace" (Diary 313).*

//////////////

*F*ollowing her profession of perpetual vows,
Sister Faustina was transferred to the city
of Vilnius, and arrived there on May 25, 1933.
She would remain there for the next three years.
In her diary, Faustina briefly reported her first
impressions of her new convent community:

> A few scattered tiny huts make up the
> large buildings of Jozefow. There are
> only eighteen sisters here. The house is
> small, but the community life is more
> intimate. All the sisters received me
> very warmly, which was for me a great
> encouragement to endure the hardships
> that lay ahead. Sister Justine had even
> scrubbed the floor in anticipation of my
> arrival (Diary 261).

Shortly after her arrival, Faustina was
deeply in prayer before the Blessed Sacrament,
asking Jesus for the appropriate graces as she
began her new position within the community
— chief gardener.

There was much that was new and challenging to Faustina at Vilnius. First of all, the rou-

tine at the convent required some getting used to. This meant adjusting to the different customs particular to her new environment. And then there was her position as chief gardener! Faustina had no idea as to where to begin with this position, as she knew practically nothing about gardening. Plus, she would have to deal with lay people in this area of work, and she was quite uncomfortable with that. Faustina's mind and soul were occupied with these worries, but God was sending someone to her so that she might be more confident in dealing with such concerns.

It was during the week of confession that an excited Faustina first saw — in person — the priest who would be her confessor, the priest she had seen in her visions, Reverend Michael Sopocko. Faustina felt comfortable in revealing her soul to this priest, including the many visions she continued to experience. She spoke to Fr. Sopocko about the first time Jesus appeared to her — two years earlier, in 1931 — to explain to her the mission he expected her to complete as the apostle and messenger of Divine Mercy:

> In the evening, when I was in my cell, I saw the Lord Jesus clad in a white garment. One hand [was] raised in the gesture of blessing, the other was touching the garment at the breast. From beneath the garment, slightly drawn aside at the

breast, there were emanating two large rays, one red, the other pale. In silence I kept my gaze fixed on the Lord, my soul was struck with awe, but also with great joy. After a while, Jesus said to me, "Paint an Image according to the pattern you see, with the signature: 'Jesus, I Trust in You.' I desire that this Image be venerated, first in your chapel, and [then] throughout the entire world.

"I promise that the soul that will venerate this Image will not perish. I also promise victory over [its] enemies already here on earth, especially at the hour of death. I Myself will defend it as My own glory....

"I desire that there be a Feast of Mercy. I want this Image, which you will paint with a brush, to be solemnly blessed on the first Sunday after Easter; that Sunday is to be the Feast of Mercy.

"I desire that priests proclaim this great mercy of Mine toward souls of sinners. Let the sinner not be afraid to approach Me. The flames of Mercy are burning Me — clamoring to be spent; I want to pour them out upon these souls" (Diary 47–50).

This was the first of many visions Faustina had in which Jesus spoke to her regarding her role in promoting Divine Mercy to the suffering world.

Fr. Sopocko was fascinated by Faustina's descriptions of her visions, specifically by Jesus' instruction to the sister that she have a painting made of the Image of the Divine Mercy. Fr. Sopocko was curious as to what this portrait would look like, so he asked a neighborhood artist to paint the image according to Sister Faustina's instruction. Fr. Sopocko also directed Faustina to ask Jesus about the significance of the rays in the vision. The Lord explained to her:

> The two rays denote Blood and Water. The pale ray stands for the Water which makes souls righteous. The red ray stands for the Blood which is the life of souls....
>
> These two rays issued forth from the very depths of My tender Mercy when My agonized Heart was opened by a lance on the Cross.
>
> These rays shield souls from the wrath of My Father. Happy is the one who will dwell in their shelter, for the just hand of God shall not lay hold of him. I desire that the first Sunday after Easter be the Feast of Mercy.
>
> Ask of my faithful servant [Father Sopocko] that, on this day, he tell the

whole world of My great Mercy; that whoever approaches the Fount of Life on this day will be granted complete remission of sins and punishment.

Mankind will not have peace until it turns with trust to My Mercy....

Proclaim that mercy is the greatest attribute of God (Diary 299–300).

Saint Faustina's mission in life was becoming clear: she was to proclaim to the world that God desired sinners and those in need of love to trust in the great mercy of the Lord and rest therein.

In union with Saint Faustina Kowalska, let us pray to the Divine Mercy:

I fly to Your mercy, Compassionate God,
who alone are good.
Although my misery is great
and my offenses are many,
I trust in Your mercy,
because You are the God of mercy;
and, from time immemorial,
it has never been heard of,
nor do heaven or earth remember,
that a soul trusting in
Your mercy has been disappointed.
O God of compassion,
You alone can justify me and
You will never reject me when I, contrite,
approach Your Merciful Heart,
where no one has ever been refused,
even if he were the greatest sinner
(Diary 1730).

O Greatly Merciful God, Infinite Goodness,
today all mankind
calls out from the abyss of its misery
to your mercy — to Your compassion,
O God; and it is with its mighty voice
of misery that it cries out.
Gracious God, do not reject the prayer
of this earth's exiles!
O Lord, Goodness
beyond our understanding,
Who are acquainted with our misery
through and through,
and know that by our own power
we cannot ascend to You,
we implore You:
anticipate us with Your grace
and keep on increasing Your mercy in us,
that we may faithfully do your holy will
all through our life and at death's hour.
Let the omnipotence of Your mercy
shield us from
the darts of our salvation's enemies,
that we may with confidence,
as Your children, await Your final coming
— that day known to You alone.
And we expect to obtain everything promised us
by Jesus in spite of all our wretchedness.
For Jesus is our Hope:
Through His merciful Heart,
as through an open gate,
we pass through to heaven
(Diary 1570).

Let us now pray the Chaplet of Divine Mercy (page 27)....

Reflection Questions

When I stop to consider the Divine, what attributes do I assign to God? What type of "personality" do I envision? Do I see a God of justice? A God of love? A God of compassion? A God of jealousy? Do I often consider the merciful aspect of God? When I do reflect on God's mercy, how is my prayer life affected? Do I find that I am more open with God, that I can tell him anything and everything in my heart in a spirit of trust, with total confidence that I am forgiven anything because of God's great mercy and his love for me?

4
Love for the Eucharist

Focus Point

////////////

As the meals we eat in our daily lives sustain us and help us to grow, so does the Eucharist, the Body of Christ, nourish us spiritually. We are called to receive Holy Communion each time we participate in the Mass. Jesus gives himself totally to each of us in the sacrament of the Eucharist, and we are bonded to our Lord in love. We are called to love through this union with Christ, and we are moved to give ourselves totally to God — to live every moment of our lives for him — just as Jesus offered himself totally to the Father in all that he said and did.

////////////

[The Lord said to me:] "Oh, how painful it is to Me that souls so seldom unite themselves to Me in Holy Communion. I wait for souls, and they are indifferent

*toward Me. I love them tenderly and sincerely, and
they distrust Me. I want to lavish My graces on them,
and they do not want to accept them. They treat Me
as a dead object, whereas My Heart is full of love and
mercy. In order that you may know at least some of
My pain, imagine the most tender of mothers who
has great love for her children, while those children
spurn her love. Consider her pain. No one is in a
position to console her. This is but a feeble image and
likeness of My love" (Diary 1447).*

////////////////

*I*t all begins with God's love: "God so loved
the world that he gave his only Son, so that
everyone who believes in him may not perish but
may have eternal life" (Jn 3:16). Jesus Christ,
God's Son, was born of the Virgin Mary, lived
among us, died, and rose from the dead. All
of this was made possible by the love of God
for his creation. God sought to unite through
Christ what had been divided through the sin of
Adam. He did not allow Adam's sin to divide
God and Man forever. No. God is love, and his
mercy is an extraordinary "face" of this love.
God's love for us is such that he sent his only
Son as a sacrifice so that this separation of God
and Man would be bridged forever.

Before he died, Jesus Christ left us the sacrament of the Eucharist, a memorial, but more
than that. In this sacrament the life, death, and
resurrection of our Lord and Savior is made

present to us, his people, in the here and now. We as God's people come together in the celebration of the Mass, as God has called us to do. Through the Mass, in communion with God and each other, we receive the body and blood of Jesus Christ. We are nourished and transformed into more Christ-like Christians by the divine substance we consume.

The Eucharist and the Divine Mercy

As it concerns the Divine Mercy, the Eucharist is essential. It permeates our hearts in love, focusing our attention on the mercy of God, making us aware that we are forgiven and loved — and that we will continue to be forgiven and loved — despite our imperfections, regardless of the number of times we sin. Sister Faustina recognized the union of the Eucharist and the Divine Mercy; she wrote in her diary of a vision she beheld in which the exposed host and the Image of the Divine Mercy (the painting) appeared in tandem:

> Once, the image was being exhibited over the altar during the Corpus Christi procession [June 20, 1935]. When the priest began to sing, the rays from the image pierced the Sacred Host and spread out all over the world. Then I heard these words: "These rays of

mercy will pass through you, just as
they have passed through this Host, and
they will go out through all the world."
At these words, profound joy invaded
my soul (Diary 441).

There is no Eucharist without mercy; that
was clear to Faustina in her vision. God's mercy
and love are the foundation of the Eucharist,
the very reason why the Father sent his Son to
gather up the lost sheep, his people.

The Eucharist Is Unity

The Eucharist involves unity. We are all
called to participate in the Mass, and we gather
there — in our churches — for a common goal:
to unite with God in love through Christ. We
are moved to unite in community by the power
of Holy Spirit, and the Fire of God's love permeates our hearts. We unite in one voice during
the eucharistic prayer. The Eucharist creates
this unity, the unity and love that each person
has for another in the community of Church,
and unity between God and Man as intended
by God in his eternal love for us. How can we
refuse him?

Sin is the source of all disunity and dishar-
mony, and we would have remained removed
from the joy and peace of God were it not
for God's own initiative, made possible by his

mercy and love, and wrought through the life and death of his Son, our Lord Jesus Christ. In his Incarnation, he became man, joining what had been separated by the misery of sin. By his death and resurrection, humanity was freed from death, united forever with the Divine. This is the joy of unity we celebrate at the Mass in the Eucharist.

Beyond the Mass

We must be aware that our celebration of the Eucharist is not limited only to the Mass. We must work towards living our entire lives in the Eucharist. Of course, everything begins with God. Any action of love we perform for God could not be so without God first giving us the grace to do so. As Jesus gave every part of himself to the Father, we must follow him. This means sacrificing our will to that of the Father. If we see someone in need of something we can give — be it a listening ear, money, and so forth — we must be charitable enough to sacrifice a luxury or pleasure and be willing to go without for love of another. Any obstacle of selfishness must be overcome.

God gives himself to us in the Mass and we are transformed when we receive him. We are transformed by love to love. With the love and mercy we have been shown, how else could we respond but to love the one who loved us first?

And what better way to show our love for him than by serving him in a tangible and concrete fashion — by serving one another. This transformation continues beyond the Mass and into the world. It grows and grows, fostering deeper love, helping to bring about the kingdom of heaven here on earth, preparing us for the eternal banquet when we depart our earthly life.

At Mass, we offer Christ up to the Father, just as our Lord did at the Last Supper and through his sacrifice on the cross. As we do this, we make our offerings to the Lord. We offer up our suffering, our talent, our love, our mercy, our fear — everything we are and everything we have we offer to God as Jesus taught us. Through this offering, in union with Jesus' sacrifice, we are united to God in the Eucharist. Faustina understood this desire to be united with her Lord and Savior very well, as she gave everything she had and all that she was for love of God. We pray with her now:

I adore You, Lord and Creator,
hidden in the Blessed Sacrament.
I adore You for all the works of Your hands,
that reveal to me so much wisdom,
goodness, and mercy, O Lord.
You have spread so much beauty over the earth,
and it tells me about Your beauty,
even though these beautiful things are
but a faint reflection of You,

Incomprehensible Beauty.
And although You have hidden Yourself
and concealed Your beauty, my eye,
enlightened by faith, reaches You,
and my soul recognizes its Creator,
its Highest Good;
and my heart is completely immersed
in prayer of adoration
(Diary 1692).

Let us now pray the Chaplet of Divine Mercy (page 27)....

Reflection Questions

Is the Eucharist an important part of my spiritual life? Do I recognize the nourishment it provides to my soul as I seek to serve God by serving his people? Does the Eucharist open my eyes to see Jesus in the people I encounter in my daily life? How might I foster a deeper devotion to the Eucharist if I feel that aspect of my spiritual life is lacking? Might I consider becoming a daily communicant for a period of one month? Might I attend a Benediction of the Blessed Sacrament available through a local parish?

5

Mercy Is the Heart of Forgiveness

Focus Point

////////////

With God as our model, we are capable of forgiveness. He has forgiven us, and we can forgive those who do us wrong. This begins with the practice of mercy. Each day we should practice at least one act of mercy so that love and forgiveness can grow inside us, and so that hardheartedness does not settle within, keeping us from a deeper love of God and each other. The Corporal and Spiritual Works of Mercy serve as an excellent list of practices for fostering mercy in our lives.

////////////

Jesus commanded me to celebrate the Feast of God's Mercy on the first Sunday after Easter.... I heard these words: "My daughter, tell the whole world about My inconceivable mercy. I desire that the Feast of

Mercy be a refuge and shelter for all souls, and especially for poor sinners. On that day the very depths of My tender mercy are open. I pour out a whole ocean of graces upon those souls who approach the fount of My mercy. The souls that will go to Confession and receive Holy Communion shall obtain complete forgiveness of sins and punishment. On that day all the divine floodgates through which grace flows are opened. Let no soul fear to draw near to Me, even though its sins be as scarlet…. The Feast of Mercy emerged from My very depths of tenderness. It is My desire that it be solemnly celebrated on the first Sunday after Easter. Mankind will not have peace until it turns to the Fount of My Mercy" (Diary 280, 699).

/////////////

*O*n April 30, 2000, the day Faustina Kowalska was canonized by Pope John Paul II, the Holy Father proclaimed that the Second Sunday of Easter would become Divine Mercy Sunday. Prior to this papal announcement, numerous parishes around the world had been celebrating Divine Mercy Sunday unofficially for a number of years. On the days prior to Divine Mercy Sunday the observance can include practicing works of mercy and participating in the sacrament of penance. On the feast day itself, the Chaplet of Divine Mercy is recited, the Image of the Divine Mercy is venerated, and Holy Communion is received. A Benediction and exposition of the Blessed Sacrament may also take place. According to the words of Jesus in Faustina's diary, "whoever approaches the Fount of Life on this day will be granted complete remission of sins and punishment" (Diary 300).

Mercy Begins With God

We are forgiven. This reality must never escape our understanding of who we are and where we stand with God. We are his beloved creation; we could never offend him to the point that he would not show us his mercy and love in forgiveness. Even as he was dying on the cross, dying for our sins, at the hands of the people he had created with love, our Lord said: "Father forgive them; for they do not know what they are doing" (Lk 23:34).

We are never beyond God's reach. Despite what we may have done in our past, regardless of the poor choices we have made, the hurtful words we have spoken, the violence to which we have turned a blind eye, the abuse we have inflicted — we are forgiven by God when we come to him in a state of sincere regret for what we have done and what we have failed to do. His mercy is unlimited and it is always available to us. We must recognize this reality.

It is imperative to our own spiritual health and to our relationships with others.

We Have Been Hurt

We have all been wronged at some time in our lives. Many of us have been injured — physically or psychologically — in a repeated fashion. We have been lied to, hit, neglected, slandered. We have had items stolen from us; we have had our hearts broken by people who manipulated us for their own selfish intentions. We seem to have every right to be angry, cynical, pessimistic, and eternally unforgiving. We may feel that hating the other, holding a grudge against them, is the only thing we can do, that it is the only power we possess in our battle against those who have wronged us.

Despite all of these "rights," and regardless of what kind of justice we feel our offender deserves, hatred and an unforgiving attitude do little to benefit either party in a situation where one person has wronged another. We are called to the higher plane of love, and we have been given a model of this love in the life of our Lord Jesus Christ. We are forgiven by God, and we are to forgive as well: "Be merciful, just as your Father is merciful" (Lk 6:36).

Freedom in Forgiveness,
Joy in Mercy

When we cling to unforgivingness, when we
hold a grudge, we are closing ourselves off from
the freedom that forgiveness brings. We can soon
become chained to our grudges and unforgivingness, and we can expend tremendous amounts
of energy blaming those who have wronged us.
This can become a habit, hardening us in anger
and blame, and isolating those close to us who
are in need of our love and attention. It is possible to create a private hell of unforgivingness.

It is not too late to foster a sense of forgiveness and mercy even if the habit of unforgivingness seems ingrained. Time must be devoted
to forgiveness and mercy in contemplation and
prayer. God took mercy on us, and in his great
love forgave our trespasses so that we would be
united with him once again. He did this through
Jesus Christ. We must recognize the Christ in
others and love accordingly. Recognizing the
Christ in others will help us to foster mercy,
and forgiveness will become a habit in our lives,
softening any hardheartedness that may have
darkened our past.

In the days preceding the Second Sunday of
Easter, it is suggested that we practice works
of mercy in preparation for the feast of Divine
Mercy. These practices will open our hearts to
the mercy and goodness of God that we will

experience so deeply on that feast day. Let us now review the Corporal and Spiritual Works of Mercy as taught by the Church:

THE CORPORAL WORKS OF MERCY

Feed the hungry
Give drink to the thirsty
Clothe the naked
Shelter the homeless
Visit the sick
Visit the imprisoned
Bury the dead

SPIRITUAL WORKS OF MERCY

Instruct the ignorant
Counsel the doubtful
Admonish the sinner
Comfort the sorrowful
Forgive injuries
Bear wrongs patiently
Pray for the living and the dead

There are people in our parishes and in our cities crying out for mercy, love, and forgiveness. We have the opportunity to provide these to them through parish-based organizations as well as on an individualized, one-to-one basis.

As we come to share ourselves with others in
a spirit of mercy and love, we will begin to feel
the shackles of fear and anger fall away from us.
The habit of mercy, of making the effort to perform at least one small act of mercy each day,
will make forgiving others come more easily to
us. Forgiveness will seem less foreign, and our
hearts will know the peace of God and bring us
ever closer to our Lord Jesus Christ, the Heart
of Mercy. Let us now pray with Faustina for a
merciful heart:

> *O Jesus, I understand that Your mercy*
> *is beyond all imagining,*
> *and therefore I ask You to make my heart so big*
> *that there will be room in it for the needs of all*
> *the souls living on the face of the earth.*
> *O Jesus, my love extends beyond the world,*
> *to the souls suffering in purgatory,*
> *and I want to exercise mercy toward them by*
> *means of indulgenced prayers.*
> *God's mercy is unfathomable and inexhaustible,*
> *just as God himself is unfathomable.*
> *Even if I were to use the strongest words there are*
> *to express this mercy of God,*
> *all this would be nothing in comparison with*
> *what it is in reality.*
> *O Jesus, make my heart sensitive to all*
> *the sufferings of my neighbor,*
> *whether of body or of soul....*
> *My Jesus, make my heart*

like unto Your merciful Heart.
Jesus, help me to go through life
doing good to everyone
(Diary 692).

Let us now pray the Chaplet of Divine Mercy (page 27)....

Reflection Questions

Do I perform the Corporal and Spiritual Works of Mercy in my own life? If not, how might I begin to do this so as to foster a level of mercy and forgiveness in my life? Might I consider joining an organization that specializes in one or more of these works of mercy, such as the Saint Vincent de Paul Society (helps to provide food, clothing, and shelter to those in need) or the Legion of Mary (visits the sick and instructs the ignorant)? Perhaps my spiritual director will have some advice as to how I can foster mercy and forgiveness in my spiritual life through the Corporal and Spiritual Works of Mercy.

6
The Chaplet

Focus Point

///////////

Jesus Christ gave a very special prayer to Saint Faustina for the benefit of everyone — the Chaplet of Divine Mercy. Jesus requested that Saint Faustina share this prayer with her community and later with the whole world. The chaplet is a prayerful request for God's mercy to enter the life of the person praying as well as the lives of those sinners being prayed for. Jesus also asked that the Hour of Great Mercy (three o'clock in the afternoon, the hour at which Christ died on Good Friday) be attended to in prayer; fittingly, the Chaplet of Divine Mercy serves as an appropriate prayer of petition for this time.

///////////

In my soul I heard these words: "This prayer will serve to appease My wrath. You will recite it for nine days, on the beads of the rosary, in the following

*manner: First of all, you will say one Our Father
and Hail Mary and the I Believe in God. Then on
the Our Father beads you will say the following
words: 'Eternal Father, I offer You the Body and
Blood, Soul and Divinity of Your dearly beloved
Son, Our Lord Jesus Christ, in atonement for our
sins and those of the whole world.' On the Hail
Mary beads you will say the following words: 'For
the sake of His sorrowful Passion have mercy on us
and on the whole world.' In conclusion, three times
you will recite these words: 'Holy God, Holy Mighty
One, Holy Immortal One, have mercy on us and on
the whole world'" (Diary 476).*

///////////

*O*ne evening in August of 1935, Sister
Faustina experienced a vision as she
prayed before the Blessed Sacrament. Before her
eyes she saw Jesus tied to a pillar, naked. Four
men began beating Jesus with whips, torturing
the Son of God. As she watched the horrible
scene unfold, Sister Faustina notes in her diary,
"My heart almost stopped at the sight of these
tortures" (445). The Lord spoke to Faustina,
saying, "I suffer even greater pain than that
which you see." It was then that Jesus revealed
to Sister Faustina the tremendous suffering he
has known by the moral impurity of mankind's
sins. Jesus gave Faustina the knowledge of the
human race in its present condition.

At that moment the vision transformed, illustrating quite clearly to Faustina what Jesus meant. Instead of four anonymous men lashing the Lord, Faustina saw priests, dignitaries, lay people, religious men and women — people of all ages and from every corner of the world — scourging Jesus. Jesus noted that the suffering he feels from the sins of others far outweighs the pain he knew during his passion and death. The vision again transformed, and now Jesus was nailed to the cross. All around him, Faustina saw people crucified. Many others were holding their crosses and still others were dragging their crosses behind them in an immense state of unhappiness. Jesus explained to Faustina:

> Do you see these souls? Those who are like Me in the pain and contempt they suffer will be like Me also in glory. And those who resemble Me less in pain and contempt will also bear less resemblance to Me in glory (Diary 446).

Jesus then asked Sister Faustina to meditate on what she had just seen and heard.

Faustina was coming to realize that the soul in tune with its suffering, in tune with the suffering of Jesus for the sake of our sins, is a soul that is open to mercy and loving toward sinners. The sins of others hurt us all, just as they cause Jesus greater pain than the agony of his own death. Understanding this reality, and feeling the pain to a lesser extent that Jesus feels so deeply, places one in deeper union with the Lord. We share his pain, and we respond as he has, with greater love for the sinner.

When Saint Faustina began to understand the suffering Jesus experienced because of the sins of the people he loved, the depth of his great mercy became apparent to her. Jesus desires to be merciful. He wants to shower his graces upon sinful humanity. But he wants sinful humanity to *be aware* of his mercy, and be open to receiving it. In order to make humanity aware of the accessibility of the Divine Mercy, Jesus gave Faustina a prayer to share with the world so that anyone could obtain this mercy.

About a month after her vision of Christ suffering at the hands of sinful humanity, Faustina experienced another vision, this one involving an angel, referred to by Faustina as "the executor of divine wrath" (Diary 474). The angel was standing on a cloud and was dressed in a dazzling robe; thunder and lightning went out from his hands and struck the earth. Seeing that the earth was in danger, Faustina begged the angel to refrain from this destruction and allow the world to do penance. It was then that she saw the Trinity in all its glory and fell silent in its presence. Faustina felt the power of Christ's grace within her soul, and she was brought before the throne of God. All throughout the vision, Faustina was in deep prayer, and she took notice of the angel's helplessness: "he could not carry out the just punishment which was rightly due for sins" (Diary 474).

As Faustina entered the chapel the next morning, she heard an interior voice telling her to recite a special prayer every time she entered the chapel. This prayer was to be prayed on ordinary rosary beads. It was at that moment that the Chaplet of Divine Mercy was introduced to Sister Faustina Kowalska, as it is laid out on page 27 and at the beginning of this chapter. Faustina was told by Jesus to teach the chaplet to her community and to the entire world. Our Lord would later inform Faustina:

> Whoever will recite [the chaplet] will receive great mercy at the hour of death. Priests will recommend it to sinners as their last hope of salvation. Even if there were a sinner most hardened, if he were to recite this chaplet only once, he would receive grace from My infinite mercy. I desire that the whole world know my infinite mercy. I desire to grant unimaginable graces to those souls who trust in My mercy (Diary 687).

It became very clear to Faustina that her mission in life would be to plead for mercy for the world. The great channel of this mercy is the Chaplet of Divine Mercy, the prayer which

Jesus told her to teach to everyone and spread to the ends of the earth.

Faustina was told to pray the chaplet as well. Beginning on Good Friday, Jesus instructed her to pray the Chaplet of Divine Mercy for the nine days preceding the feast of Divine Mercy, the Sunday that follows Easter. Jesus promised the Secretary of Divine Mercy: "By this novena, I will grant every possible grace to souls" (Diary 796).

According to Sister Faustina's diary, Jesus requested that prayer and meditation on his passion be devoted to the three o'clock hour of each afternoon in remembrance of his death on the cross. Jesus explained to Sister Faustina that the hour of three o'clock is the ideal time to obtain mercy for oneself and for others because as the hour of Christ's death on the cross, it was the hour of grace for the whole world — mercy triumphed over justice. Jesus asked that the attempt be made during this three o'clock hour to make the Stations of the Cross, attend to adoration of the Blessed Sacrament, or simply pray in quiet. This hour also serves as an appropriate time to pray the Chaplet of Divine Mercy.

O Lord, where will we hide
on the day of Your anger?
Without You we are a lost and broken people.
You are the source of life that we need;
You are the fountain of mercy

without whom we are nothing.
Why do we continue to push You away
when we need You so much?
You call out to us in love and
we are moved to answer.
We are moved to take refuge
in the shelter of Your mercy.
See the multitude that approaches You now,
singing hymns of praise for the mercy
You have rained upon us.
Lord, You do not forget us in our need;
turn Your face to us now.
Lord Jesus Christ, we love You!

Let us now pray the Chaplet of Divine Mercy (page 27)....

Reflection Questions

How is my understanding of God's mercy developing as I read the accounts of Saint Faustina's visions? How might further prayer and meditation on Christ's passion and death help to foster a deeper appreciation for Christ's immense mercy and love for me and for all sinners? What methods of prayer and meditation might I incorporate into my spiritual regimen as concerns the Hour of Great Mercy, each day at three o'clock?

7

Trust in Mercy

Focus Point

////////////

We are called to trust in the mercy of God. Jesus asks us, in Scripture and through Saint Faustina, to trust wholly in his mercy, love, and guidance. Saint Faustina gained a greater appreciation for the love and mercy of God during her intense periods of suffering. The Lord was merciful to her, providing the necessary graces that made her suffering bearable. Through her suffering, Faustina was brought closer to God by depending on his mercy more and more. We are called to do the same; we are called to abandon our lives of worry and self-reliance, and give ourselves completely to God, for he has promised to provide everything we need.

////////////

[Jesus said to me:] "Write: I am Thrice Holy, and I detest the smallest sin. I cannot love a soul that is stained with sin; but when it repents, there is no limit

*to My generosity toward it. My Mercy embraces and
justifies it. With My Mercy, I pursue sinners along
all their paths, and My Heart rejoices when they turn
to Me. I forget the bitterness with which they fed My
Heart and I rejoice at their return.*

*"Tell sinners that no one shall escape My Hand; if
they run away from My merciful Heart, they will fall
into My Just Hands. Tell sinners that I am always
waiting for them, that I listen intently to the beating
of their heart…when will it beat for Me? Write, that
I am speaking to them through their remorse of conscience, through their failures and sufferings, through
thunderstorms, through the voice of the Church"
(Diary 1728).*

///////////

On September 19, 1936, Sister Faustina
was sent to a lung specialist. Faustina had
been ill for some time, and her state was becoming worse. Before long, her sleep was greatly
disturbed, and she was awakened several times
a night by sharp pains. All this she endured
patiently, though she expected the hour of her
death to arrive shortly.

Faustina had been left greatly weakened by
her sufferings, too weak to participate in daily
Mass. She was in fact very surprised that she
remained alive after so much suffering and
began to wonder, since her hour of death had
not yet arrived, how great the suffering was

when death did arrive. During her intense suffering at this time, the Lord visited his servant with the request that Faustina tell the whole world of his infinite mercy and that the Sunday after Easter serve as the feast of Divine Mercy. The Lord asked this of Faustina on at least fifteen separate occasions.

The fact that Jesus spoke continually of his mercy to Faustina, particularly at those times when she was in the midst of very painful suffering, made her realize to a greater degree that periods of suffering are opportune moments to rely more and more upon the mercy of God, and thereby deepen the union between servant and Master. It was possible, in fact, to be joyful in suffering, to be happy in one's dependence and growing trust on the mercy of God in times of pain and suffering.

Our Freedom

Our God is not heartless and cruel. He is not seeking to "trip us up." In fact, God seeks to strengthen us in our weakness, giving us his grace when we face life's most intimidating obstacles. This was the case with Faustina during the time of her suffering. Faustina tried very hard to work in her community and serve just as the other sisters did. On one occasion, Faustina was working in the fields with the sun bearing down on her. But after she called out to Jesus for his mercy, the clouds in the sky swept in front of the sun, providing the tired sister some much-needed relief.

God gives us his grace, but he also has given us freedom, and we do have the freedom to refuse God's love. God has given us the Ten Commandments; we have the guidelines by which to live a life in accordance with God's will, but our freedom to say "yes" or "no" to this will is completely our own. We can seek God's help in our life, or we can seek to avoid it. The choice is ours. But we should never live under the impression that because we have done something terrible to offend our Lord or chosen to avoid God and his love for an extended length of time, that we are incapable of ever regaining his favor. It takes just a spark of trust — a spark the Lord gladly provides the sinner — in the mercy of God to start anew with a clean slate. Just as he did in the Gospel of Luke, the Lord constantly calls out to us: "Let the little children come to me … for it is such as these that the kingdom of God belongs" (18:16). We are all God's children, and he loves each of us dearly.

Trust in Mercy, Do Not Worry

Many of us spend a significant portion of our lives in worry. We worry what tomorrow will bring, we worry if our children will be safe at school, we worry about our job security, we worry about sickness, and we worry about death. So much of our mental energy is devoted to worrying about those things over which we have such little control. We sometimes feel so small and alone in the face of the unknown, and our minds swim in fear and anxiety. We have all experienced worry and we are oftentimes at a loss as to what we can do to decrease the amount of worry in our lives.

Jesus asked Faustina on several occasions to tell the world that trust in God's mercy is the key to a strong Christian life of peace and joy and happiness. These words are echoed throughout Scripture, as we read the words of Jesus in the Gospel of Matthew:

> Therefore I tell you, do not worry about your life, what you will eat or what you will drink, or about your body, what you will wear. Is not life more than food, and the body more than clothing? Look at the birds of the air; they neither sow nor reap nor gather into barns, and yet your heavenly Father feeds them. Are you not of more value than they? (…)
>
> Therefore do not worry, saying, "What will we eat?" or "What will we drink" or "What will we wear?" (…) Strive first for the kingdom of God and his righteousness, and all these things will be given to you as well.

So do not worry about tomorrow, for
tomorrow will bring worries of its own
(6:25–26, 31, 33–34).

We are told not to worry; trust in God is the
key to peace in one's life. The act of trusting
completely in God, in his mercy, throughout
our lives can seem so imposing and so very
difficult. Many of us rely only on ourselves,
saying such things as, "I'm the only person I
can trust" and "I've been let down too many
times by people I trusted to ever trust again."
It is time to trust again. It is time to trust in
God. Trusting only in ourselves does not lend
itself to peace; its end is isolation, misery, and
anxiety. To trust in no one leaves no window
open for love to shine into our lives. We must
learn to trust in God. Through this total reliance on God, we will come to love our Lord
more deeply than ever before, keeping nothing
from him, and allowing him to love us and all
our imperfections.

We must pray constantly to God for the grace
to trust totally in his mercy. Without prayer, we
risk becoming cynical and angry, relying only
on ourselves. Loneliness and fear are certain
to follow this closed-hearted approach to life.
Love cannot bloom in such soil. Reliance on
God opens our hearts to his love and mercy,
and the love and mercy of others. Our own love
increases by our experience of this love and

mercy, and our hearts cannot become hard-
ened when they are open, trusting, loving, and
"mercy filled."

> *O Blood and Water,*
> *which gushed forth from the Heart of Jesus*
> *as a fount of mercy for us,*
> *I trust in You!*
> (Diary 84).

Let us now pray the Chaplet of Divine
Mercy (page 27)....

Reflection Questions

Is there a person in my life who has shown
me mercy when I needed it the most? How did
I feel when I received that person's mercy and
forgiveness? Does imagining the way I felt then
aid me in my prayer and reflection on the great
mercy and forgiveness God has shown me
— and continues to show me — throughout
my life? Where are those places in my life that
are in need of greater mercy? Who is calling
out for my mercy? Might I pray that God open
my eyes to the places and people in need of my
love and mercy when I encounter them in my
daily life?

8
The Importance of Reconciliation

Focus Point

////////////

Jesus calls us to participate in the sacrament of penance. He desires that we open our hearts to him and allow him to heal the brokenness within. We have sinned against the Lord, but his forgiveness abides forever, without limit. The mercy Saint Faustina proclaims throughout her diary can be ours if we only respond to Christ's call. Let us examine our conscience and take responsibility for the wrongs we have committed. Let us bring our sins to the Lord with an attitude of remorse for what we have done. Let us experience his mercy in the sacrament of penance.

////////////

Today the Lord said to me, "Daughter, when you go to confession, to this fountain of My mercy, the Blood and Water which came forth from My Heart always flows down upon your soul and ennobles it. Every time you go to confession, immerse yourself entirely in My mercy, with great trust, so that I may pour the bounty of My grace upon your soul. When you approach the confessional, know this, that I Myself am waiting there for you. I am only hidden by the priest, but I myself act in your soul. Here the misery of the soul meets the God of mercy. Tell souls that from this fount of mercy souls draw graces solely with the vessel of trust. If their trust is great, there is no limit to My generosity" (Diary 1602).

////////////////

Sister Faustina prayed frequently for sinners, asking the Lord to grant them contrition and repentance. She also called out to all souls in her periods of prayer. Faustina would implore all souls not to fear God, but to put their trust in him completely, and come to know his everlasting mercy.

We have offended God with our sins, and there is a need for healing. As sinners in need of God's mercy, we can approach our Lord in trust through the sacrament of penance. Faustina prays in heaven for us now that we will seek God through this wonderful sacrament:

O Jesus, eternal Truth, our Life,
I call upon You and I beg
Your mercy for poor sinners.
O Sweetest Heart of my Lord,

full of pity and unfathomable mercy,
I plead with you for poor sinners…. O Jesus!
I desire to bring all sinners to
Your feet that they may glorify
Your mercy throughout endless ages
(Diary 72).

We are fortunate to have such abiding inter-cession to our Lord through Saint Faustina. By her prayers, and through the grace of God, we are moved to reconcile with the Father through the sacrament of penance.

A Guide to the Sacrament of Penance

PRAYER FOR RECONCILIATION

Holy Lord, almighty Father,
look upon me, your servant,
who is overwhelmed
by the storms of this world
and in tears pleads guilty
to all manner of transgressions.
Have pity on my sighs and tears,
and call me back from darkness into light.
Heal me when I confess,
save me when I do penance,
and help my wounds to become whole.
Let the enemy have no more power
over my spirit.
Graciously receive my confession, purify me,
and bring me back to your grace,

through this reconciling sacrament
through which
I give thanks to your holy Name. Amen.

At this point, an examination of conscience is appropriate. Here is an example of the process of examination of conscience:

1. Find a quiet place to sit or kneel.
2. Review your life — those things you have done and those things you have not done — since your last confession.
3. Reflect on the Ten Commandments. To the best of your memory, call to mind any sins against the commandments. Is my heart centered on God, or do I worship things (money, power, and so on) more than him? Do I keep holy the Sabbath? Do I seek to speak only the truth, and avoid gossip and slander? Do I seek to promote the values of life and battle against those forces that threaten the innocent? Have I taken something that did not belong to me?
4. Reflect on Jesus' commandment to love your neighbor as yourself (Mt 22:34–40). Do I truly love my neighbors? Do I ever use my neighbors as a means to an end? Do I contribute to the happiness of my family? Do I aid the poor and unfortunate? Do I seek to promote peace and understanding in race relations? Have I been compassionate and

merciful to those who have wronged me? Have I allowed fear and anxiety to keep me from acting with love towards others?

After a sufficient examination of conscience, the penitent enters the confessional, makes the Sign of the Cross, and is invited by the priest to trust in the mercy of God. The priest might welcome the penitent by saying, "May the Lord Jesus Christ welcome you. Our Lord came to call sinners to his merciful heart. Have trust in him." Prior to the confession of sins, the priest may choose to cite scriptural references regarding the Lord providing what we seek from him (in this case forgiveness), for example: "Ask, and it will be given you; search, and you will find; knock, and the door will be opened for you" (Mt 7:7).

The sins of the penitent are confessed to the priest. The priest may aid the penitent in this process, giving advice or asking questions for the sake of specificity. The priest then imposes penance on the penitent and requests that the penitent express sorrow for his sins by reciting an act of contrition, for example:

O my God, I am truly sorry for my sins with all of my heart. In choosing to do wrong and failing to do good, I have sinned against you whom I should love above all things. I firmly intend, with your help, to do penance, to sin no more, and to avoid all paths that might lead me to sin. In his great love, your Son, our Lord and Savior Jesus Christ, died for us. In his name, my God, have mercy on me. Amen.

Following the act of contrition, the confessor says the following words:

God, the Father of mercies, through the death and resurrection of his Son, has reconciled the world to himself and sent the Holy Spirit among us for the forgiveness of sins; through the ministry of the Church, may God give you pardon and peace, and I absolve you from your sins in the name of the Father, and of the Son, and of the Holy Spirit.

The reconciled penitent is dismissed by the priest with the words: "The Lord has freed you from your sins. Go in peace." Following the confession, the reconciled penitent will perform the penance as directed by the confessor. The reconciled penitent may also say a prayer after confession, for example:

Lord Jesus Christ,
I have confessed all my sins
to the best of my effort.
From the depth of my heart,
I have tried to make a good confession.

I know that you have forgiven me for,
as Saint Faustina has reminded me,
your heart is full of love and mercy,
and it calls out to all
who have sinned to reconcile with
you in this great sacrament.
I love you, Jesus;
I will try to keep from sinning again
and will try to love you more each day. Amen.

The experience of the sacrament of penance can be a liberating experience, a reunion of the soul with the peace and love of God. There is great healing in this sacrament. We take responsibility for our actions and bring them humbly to the mercy of the Father. By his love and mercy, we come to know forgiveness, and our desire to love God and neighbor is renewed. Saint Faustina recognized the sacrament of penance as the meeting place of Jesus and souls. This is the meeting place of love and healing. We are called to enter it.

Happy are those whose
transgression is forgiven,
whose sin is covered.
Happy are those to whom
the LORD imputes no iniquity,
and in whose spirit there is no deceit.

While I kept silence,
my body wasted away
through my groaning all day long.

For day and night your hand
was heavy upon me;
my strength was dried up
as by the heat of summer.

Then I acknowledged my sin to you,
and I did not hide my iniquity;
I said, "I will confess my
transgressions to the LORD,"
and you forgave the guilt of my sin.

Therefore let all who are faithful
offer prayer to you. Amen (Ps 32:1–6).

Let us now pray the Chaplet of Divine Mercy (page 27)....

Reflection Questions

Do I participate in the sacrament of penance on a regular basis? If I do not, what fears, anxieties, or other issues prevent me from doing so? Do I find it difficult to forgive myself? If so, might I pray that mercy be made manifest in me to a greater degree so that I may come to love myself despite the fact that I sometimes fail? How does my understanding of God's desire to forgive me affect my dealings with those people who have wronged me in my life? Do I find it difficult to forgive others? If so, might regular participation in the sacrament of penance help me to become more merciful?

9
Love for Mary

Focus Point

////////////

Faustina had a very special relationship with the Blessed Virgin Mary. In a deep spiritual sense, Mary became Faustina's mother and Faustina became Mary's daughter. During visions in which she appeared to Faustina, Mary directed her daughter to grow in virtue through the practice of humility, purity, and love of God. In our own lives, we strive to grow in love by practicing these virtues. Mary serves as the ideal model of humility, purity, and love of God. This reality is echoed throughout Scripture and is inherent to Mary's role as the Mother of God.

////////////

Before Holy Communion I saw the Blessed Mother inconceivably beautiful. Smiling at me She said to me, "My daughter, at God's command I am to be, in a special and exclusive way your Mother; but I desire that you, too, in a special way, be My child.

"I desire, My dearly beloved daughter, that you practice the three virtues that are dearest to Me — and most pleasing to God. The first is humility, humility, and once again humility; the second virtue, purity; the third virtue, love of God. As My daughter, you must especially radiate with these virtues." When the conversation ended, She pressed me to Her Heart and disappeared. When I regained the use of my senses, my heart became so wonderfully attracted to these virtues; and I practice them faithfully. They are as though engraved in my heart (Diary 1414–1415).

///////////

*D*uring a novena to the Blessed Virgin Mary, Sister Faustina greeted the Madonna each day by praying the Hail Mary one thousand times. As we read above, Faustina and the Blessed Virgin shared a very special, personal relationship, mirroring that of a mother and daughter. Mary guided Faustina in her spiritual life, directing her to strive for silence and humility as the sister prepared for Christmas in 1936. Humility was a goal laid out for Sister Faustina by the Mother of God, as was purity and love of God — each trait an immediately identifiable facet of the Blessed Virgin herself.

Humility

To be humble is to recognize the low state of one's person in the presence of God. To be humble is to understand that there is a God, and we are not him. To be humble is to know our place as servant, and to recognize the authority of the Master.

The epitome of the humble creature is Mary, the Mother of God. From the first time we meet her in the gospel story — when she says to the angel, "Here I am, the servant of the Lord; let it be with me according to your word" (Lk 1:38) — we see a woman without a hint of arrogance or pride. God requested her participation in the salvation of the world and Mary cooperated wholeheartedly in the Incarnation, giving her consent with an interior freedom that knew to choose the will of God over any individual selfishness that may have objected to the divine plan.

Mary is a servant of the Lord in the truest sense: whatever he wills she will accept. Mary presents her entire life to the Lord as a gift of service and obedience. She is the creature, he is the Creator. The simplicity of this reality, modeled by Mary, escapes the most intelligent of academics, but it is engraved in the hearts of the greatest of saints.

Purity

On a particular day in 1929, while she was at Mass, Faustina received a special gift:

> Jesus appeared suddenly at my side clad in a white garment with a golden girdle around His waist, and He said to me, "I give you eternal love that your purity may be untarnished and as a sign that you will never be subject to temptations against purity." Jesus took off His golden cincture and tied it around my waist.
>
> Since then I have never experienced any attacks against this virtue, either in my heart or in my mind. I later understood that this was one of the greatest graces which the Most Holy Virgin Mary had obtained for me, as for many years I had been asking this grace of Her. Since that time I have experienced an increasing devotion to the Mother of God (Diary 40).

Through the intercession of Mary, Faustina was given the gift she had asked for: strength in resisting temptations against purity.

Of course, Mary is the model of purity. She is the Ever-Virgin, wholly devoted to the Father, completely trusting in his will. At the time of the Annunciation, Mary did question how it was possible that she was pregnant, considering her state of virginity, but she never doubted the power of God to make the impossible possible. Mary was the perfect and pure vessel through which God would enter the world. Her place in salvation was determined at the outset of creation, as was the necessity of her purity and virginity. By Mary's aid, Faustina was graced to know the depths of purity in her own life.

Love of God

Perhaps no creature has ever known the mercy of God to such depths as Mary, the Mother of Mercy. She was the humble creature called to participate in the mystery of the Incarnation. God loved her so much that she was born free of the stain of original sin so that Jesus Christ would grow in a womb pure and clean. God's love for Mary endures, from before she was born, to her assumption into heaven, to this very day, and forever after. This humble and loving woman made her whole life a "yes" to the will of God, and lived her life totally for him in union with his divine will.

Because God loves her so much, he cannot refuse her requests when she appeals for his graces on our behalf. Mary is our loving intercessor, and any intention she brings to God from our prayers to her he will not decline. Mary sees us in our need, and she has mercy upon us. She seeks to come to our assistance, just as she came to the aid of those in need in the Gospel of John:

> On the third day there was a wedding in Cana of Galilee, and the mother of Jesus was there. Jesus and his disciples had also been invited to the wedding. When the wine gave out, the mother of Jesus said to him, "They have no wine." and Jesus said to her, "Woman, what concern is that to you and to me? My hour has not yet come." His mother said to the servants, "Do whatever he tells you." Now standing there were six stone water jars for the Jewish rites of purification, each holding twenty or thirty gallons. Jesus said to them, "Fill the jars with water." And they filled them up to the brim. He said to them, "Now draw some out, and take it to the chief steward." So they took it. When the steward tasted the water that had become wine, and did not know where it came from (though the servants who had drawn the water knew), the steward called the bridegroom and said to him, "Everyone serves the good wine first, and then the inferior wine after the guests have become drunk. But you have kept the good wine until now." Jesus did this, the first of his signs, in Cana of

Galilee, and revealed his glory; and his disciples believed in him (2:1–11).

The Father cannot refuse the Blessed Virgin, the woman he chose to be the mother of Jesus, the Mother of peace, and the Mother of mercy. Mary is our model of humility, purity, and love of God. God has commanded us in the Gospel of Matthew 22:37, "You shall love the Lord your God with all your heart, and with all your soul, and with all your mind." Mary's entire existence was directed toward this goal; she seeks to guide us there as well.

O Mary, today a terrible sword
has pierced Your holy soul.
Except for God, no one knows of Your suffering.
Your soul does not break; it is brave,
because it is with Jesus.
Sweet Mother, unite my soul to Jesus,
because it is only then that I will be able
to endure all trials and tribulations,
and only in union with Jesus
will my little sacrifices be pleasing to God.
Sweetest Mother, continue to teach me
about the interior life.
May the sword of suffering never break me.
O pure Virgin,
pour courage into my heart and guard it
(Diary 915).

Let us now pray the Chaplet of Divine Mercy (page 27)....

Reflection Questions

What does Mary teach me about humility? How can fostering humility in my life lead me to a deeper relationship with God? How does Mary model purity to me? How does this purity affect my understanding of my body as a gift from God to be used to glorify his holy name? How can I increase my love for God in my devotion to Mary? Might praying the rosary on a regular basis aid me in giving my will over to the Father and trusting in his divine will more completely, as Mary did with her whole being during her entire life?

10
The Mission

Focus Point

////////////

Faustina's mission in life was to proclaim the mercy of God as revealed to her in prayer and visions. She did this dutifully by being loving and merciful in her own life, by keeping a diary devoted to the Divine Mercy, and by teaching the world the Chaplet of Divine Mercy as Jesus had directed her to do. As baptized believers, we too have a duty to proclaim the gospel message in our words and in our actions. We are called to trust in the Divine Mercy, and to live a Christian life with the faith that the grace of God will help us to overcome any obstacle that obstructs us from serving the will of the Father.

////////////

My Jesus, I will now strive to give honor and glory to Your Name, doing battle till the day on which You yourself will say, enough! Every soul You have

*entrusted to me, Jesus, I will try to aid with prayer
and sacrifice, so that Your grace can work in them.
O great lover of souls, my Jesus, I thank You for this
immense confidence with which You have deigned to
place souls in our care. O you days of work and of
monotony, you are not monotonous to me at all, for
each moment brings me new graces and opportunity
to do good (Diary 245).*

///////////////

Because of her worsening health, Faustina
was sent to the sanatorium in Pradnik
for a three-month treatment in December of
1936. Faustina felt anxious about being away
from her community, but Jesus assured her
that he would be with her, "always and everywhere," and that this period of solitude was in
accordance with his will "so that I Myself may
form your heart according to My future plans"
(Diary 797).

Throughout her days of suffering in
Pradnik, Faustina noticed how little the
patients spoke of God, and how much they
discussed and laughed about every other topic
but their Creator. Faustina prayed frequently
during her stay at the sanatorium, but she felt
deep sadness for those patients who seemed to
have no relationship at all with Jesus. Despite
this sadness and some loneliness from a lack of
visitors, Faustina took great comfort in know-

ing Jesus more and more through her suffering, and she began to anticipate her coming death with great excitement.

But before she would enter into new life through death, Sister Faustina was continually directed to proclaim — through her writing — the bottomless mercy of Christ. Jesus told her: "Write: Before I come as a just Judge, I first open wide the door of My mercy. He who refuses to pass through the door of My mercy must pass through the door of My justice ..." (Diary 1146). Throughout this period of suffering and recording the messages of the Divine Mercy in her diary, Faustina committed herself to her duty and mission with great focus, moving Jesus to say to her: "These efforts of yours, My daughter, are pleasing to Me; they are the delight of My Heart" (Diary 1176).

Mission of Baptized Believers

As baptized believers, we all have the mission to proclaim the gospel message. We have the duty to preach that way of life which leads to life eternal in the presence of God. We realize that we cannot save the souls of others. That has already been accomplished through the sacrifice of Christ on the cross. Even when a heart is seemingly converted to life in Christ by our words or actions, we are not ultimately responsible — only God converts the sinner.

We are not only called to preach the gospel, we are also directed to live it. We must live Christ's love in word *and* action. If our actions are not rooted in the gospel message, but we preach the gospel in spite of this, our message is empty and without impact. But when a person in need of a life in the peace and guidance of Christ witnesses a baptized believer who preaches *and* lives the gospel message — when this happiness is radiated by such a believer — a person in need sees a way of life that is appealing, and this person is moved by God's grace to start on the path to life in Christ.

As Christians who preach and live the gospel message, we are baptized believers with a mission to evangelize. We are called to commitment in our duty to Christ's direction, just as Saint Faustina would not cease in her devoted efforts to proclaim the mercy of God with every amount of energy she could muster. We are called to service by the Lord, though not necessarily success. Like many of the Old Testament prophets and numerous saints in our Christian tradition, we may not be alive to see the fruits of our labor as servants of God. We must not be so concerned with our perceptions of success and failure in regard to our mission and duty to Christ's gospel message that we abandon our duty in a state of discouragement. No. We must faithfully serve despite the fears and obstacles we encounter. Our faithfulness and commitment to

the Lord is the goal to which we should direct
our energy and attention.

"Follow Me with All Your Heart"

When Jesus called his first disciples, he simply said, "Follow me" (Mk 2:14). The earliest
disciples saw a teacher, a man of power, a man
of peace, and they were moved to follow him.
These disciples were so resolute in their decision to follow Jesus that they left their previous lives and did not look back (see Mk 1:20).
They had no idea what obstacles and dangers
they would face due to this decision to abandon their old lives for an unknown future, but
their trust and faith told them that they had
found someone special — they had "found the
Messiah" (Jn 1:41).

Once a person has found the highest good, it
only makes sense that that person would want
to remain in the presence of the highest good
and invest oneself entirely in it. That is the way
we feel when we come to know the love and
peace of God, is it not? Once we have encountered Jesus Christ, the Divine Mercy, are we
not moved to abandon our previous lives and
follow him, just as the first disciples did? We are
not asked to cry for our past and our previous
state of blindness. We are called to follow. The
past has no hold on us once we have seen the
possibility of the future. The shackles of what

was fall from us the moment we turn our gaze in the direction of Jesus.

After we begin to follow Jesus, his call to discipleship intensifies. Like he did for Faustina, he gives us graces to resist temptation and to remain resolute in our faith. We are called to follow him at first, and we do, but as we become stronger in our love for him we are called to lead others into his loving presence by our life as Christians. As Jesus explained:

> No one after lighting a lamp hides it under a jar, or puts it under a bed, but puts in on a lampstand, so that those who enter may see the light. For nothing is hidden that will not be disclosed, nor is anything secret that will not become known and come to light (Lk 8:16–17).

By Christ's Incarnation and his sacrifice on the cross, sinful humanity was reunited with its Creator. The Incarnation and the crucifixion are tremendous reminders of God's great mercy for each one of us. It is up to us to trust in God's mercy as we seek to do his will. We will suffer setbacks and face obstacles in our efforts, but we must pray for the grace to remain determined in our mission to proclaim and live the gospel message. As Faustina experienced in her own life, God will see us through our difficulties if we place our trust wholly in his mercy.

O God, show me Your mercy
according to the compassion
of the Heart of Jesus.
Hear my sighs and entreaties,
And the tears of a contrite heart.

O Omnipotent, ever-merciful God,
Your compassion is never exhausted.
Although my misery is as vast as the sea,
I have complete trust in the mercy of the Lord.

O Eternal Trinity, yet ever-gracious God,
Your compassion is without measure,
and so I trust in the sea of Your mercy,
and sense You, Lord,
though a veil holds me aloof.

May the omnipotence
of Your mercy, O Lord,
Be glorified all over the world.
May veneration of it never cease.
Proclaim, my soul, God's mercy with fervor.

Let us now pray the Chaplet of Divine Mercy (page 27)....

Reflection Questions

In what ways do I evangelize? Might I make a conscious effort to do so through small acts of love and mercy directed to those people I encounter in my daily life? Perhaps reading the Bible on a daily basis would aid me in finding the right words when I discuss the gospel message with others. Might I consider joining a parish group — such as the Legion of Mary — in my effort to spread the Word of God to those people who are in need of its comfort and its promise of hope and peace?

11
A Special Prayer
for Faustina

Focus Point

////////////

Toward the end of her life, Sister Faustina was directed by Jesus to pray a special novena during the nine days preceding the feast of Divine Mercy. According to Jesus' request, she was to pray for a different group of souls each day. In her novena prayer she brought these souls to Jesus so that they would experience the love and mercy that only the Lord can provide. In our own lives, we can seek God's mercy through the intercession of Saint Faustina, who continues her mission to serve Christ by bringing souls to his merciful heart.

////////////

[Jesus said to me:] "I desire that during these nine days you bring souls to the fount of My mercy, that

they may draw therefrom strength and refreshment and whatever graces they need in the hardships of life and, especially, at the hour of death.

"On each day you will bring to My Heart a different group of souls, and you will immerse them in this ocean of My mercy, and I will bring all these souls into the house of My Father. You will do this in this life and in the next. I will deny nothing to any soul whom you will bring to the fount of My mercy. On each day you will beg My Father, on the strength of My bitter Passion, for graces for these souls."

I answered, "Jesus, I do not know how to make this novena or which souls to bring first into Your Most Compassionate Heart." Jesus replied that He would tell me which souls to bring each day into His Heart (Diary 1209).

///////////////

A lmost eighteen months before she would die, Sister Faustina was asked by Jesus to make a unique novena. Beginning on Good Friday, 1937, and continuing through the following Saturday (the day before the feast of Divine Mercy), Faustina was to pray for a specific group of souls each day, as dictated by Jesus. Each group of souls was to be brought forth to drink from the fount of Christ's mercy so that these souls would gain the graces they needed to endure the "hardships of life and, especially, at the hour of death" (Diary 1209).

On this eleventh day of prayer with Saint Faustina Kowalska, as we reflect on those groups of souls that Jesus desired to be led by Faustina each day to his fountain of grace, let us pray for those people in our world in need of the grace of God's mercy, that they open their hearts to his love and trust in his divine will.

First Day

On the first day of the Novena to the Divine Mercy, Faustina was asked to bring to Jesus all of humanity, particularly the sinners, so that they might be plunged into the ocean of God's mercy.

Dear Jesus,
have mercy on all sinners,
all of mankind, and forgive
all the wrongs that we have done.

Jesus, you died on the cross for our sins.
Please show us your mercy
and pour your love upon us.

May we praise your merciful heart
and glorify your holy name now and always.
We commit our lives to you,
we trust our lives to you.

Give us the graces
we need to accomplish your will.
We thank you for your passion,
death, and resurrection,
we thank you for your pardon,

and we thank you for your gift
of eternal life. Amen.

Second Day

On the second day of the Novena to the Divine Mercy, Faustina brought to Jesus the souls of priests and religious. Jesus deeply loves this group, as they provided him strength in the suffering of his passion. Jesus also mentions that mercy flows through this group to all of humanity.

Bless the souls of priests and religious,
I pray you, dearest Lord.
Keep them, for they guide
others along the path to salvation.
Keep them, for they are in the world,
though not of the world;
when these holy priests and
religious face temptation,
shelter them in your heart.
Keep them, and comfort them in hours
of suffering and loneliness.
When they become discouraged,
O Lord, help them to remember
their full reliance is on you.
Keep in mind their human frailty.
Keep them pure in their thoughts,
words, and actions.
Bless them, O Lord. Amen.

Third Day

On the third day of the Novena to the Divine Mercy, Jesus asked that all faithful souls be brought to his ocean of mercy. He explained to Faustina that they were the souls that consoled him as he walked the road to Calvary.

Lord Jesus Christ,
impart your mercy and blessings
upon those souls
who trust in you and strive to do your will.
Protect those devoted souls
who seek only to love
and be loved by you. Amen.

Fourth Day

On the fourth day of the Novena to the Divine Mercy, Jesus asked that those souls who did not know him be brought to his ocean of mercy. He told Sister Faustina that the ardor for the faith that would come to blossom in these people comforted his heart.

Generous Lord,
rain your graces upon those souls
who do not know your saving name.
Merciful Teacher,
shine the brilliance of your love
upon those souls
who have known only darkness.
Compassionate Savior,

look upon the lost and lonely pagan souls
and grant them the mercy
that your devout and faithful souls
have come to know in you. Amen.

Fifth Day

On the fifth day of the Novena to the Divine Mercy, Jesus asked Sister Faustina to bring him the souls of heretics and schismatics so that they might be immersed in his ocean of mercy. Jesus desires that these souls be returned to unity with the Church, and by their arrival his passion is soothed.

Almighty God,
have mercy on all those
who have persisted in their errors
and chosen what is less than you.
Merciful Shepherd,
lead the souls of all
heretics and schismatics
back into your fold,
into the light of your love,
and may they never
know darkness again. Amen.

Sixth Day

On the sixth day of the Novena to the Divine Mercy, Faustina brought to the ocean of Christ's mercy those meek and humble souls and the souls of little children. Jesus saw such souls as angels on the earth, keeping vigil at his altars.

O Lord Jesus,
you favor humble souls with your confidence.
Fill the souls of the meek and humble,
and all the souls of little children,
with your mercy.
We pray to you this day
to open the gates of heaven to all
the meek and humble souls,
and to all the souls of little children. Amen.

Seventh Day

On the seventh day of the Novena to the Divine Mercy, Faustina brought to Jesus those souls who especially venerate and glorify his mercy. Christ views these souls as the living images of his merciful heart.

O Lord,
shower your mercy upon those souls
who glorify your immense mercy,
in word and deed,
for love of you. Amen.

Eighth Day

On the eighth day of the Novena to the Divine Mercy, the souls of purgatory were brought to the ocean of Christ's mercy. By his mercy, Christ requested that all the indulgences of his Church be offered toward their debt.

Merciful Jesus, I pray to you,
through the kindness of your heart,
take pity on the souls imprisoned in purgatory.
Dear Lord,
recall that these are your friends,
your children, whom you have redeemed
by your saving hand.
Loving Savior,
we pray to you this day,
show mercy and remit the remainder
of their suffering. Amen.

Ninth Day

On the ninth and final day of the Novena to the Divine Mercy, Jesus asked that Faustina bring to the ocean of mercy all lukewarm souls. By his mercy, Jesus desired to inflame these souls with zeal and love for life in Christ.

Merciful Lord,
by the flame of your love,
melt the ice that surrounds the hearts
of all cool souls.
Loving God,
fill their hungry hearts
with the manna you provide
so generously to your people in need. Amen.

By the prayers of this novena, we have prayed in union with Jesus Christ. His intentions are our own; may all the souls for whom we have prayed come to his ocean of mercy according to his will.

Out of the depths
I cry to you, O LORD.
LORD, hear my voice!
Let your ears be attentive
to the voice of my supplications!

If you, O LORD,
should mark iniquities,
LORD, who could stand?
But there is forgiveness with you,
so that you may be revered.

I wait for the LORD, my soul waits,
and in his word I hope;
my soul waits for the LORD
more than those who watch
for the morning.

O Israel, hope in the LORD!
For with the LORD
there is steadfast love,
and with him
is great power to redeem.
It is he who will redeem Israel
from all its iniquities (Ps 130).

Let us now pray the Chaplet of Divine Mercy (page 27)....

Reflection Questions

Saint Faustina wrote in her diary: "My mission will not come to an end upon my death, but will begin. O doubting souls, I will draw aside for you the veils of heaven to convince you of God's goodness, so that you will no longer continue to wound with your distrust the sweetest Heart of Jesus. God is Love and Mercy" (Diary 281). Do I pray for the intercession of Saint Faustina in my life and in the lives of others? What acts of mercy do I incorporate in my daily life to make known to others the mercy of Jesus Christ?

12
Suffering

Focus Point

////////////

We all experience suffering in our lives. There can be a tendency toward selfishness in suffering and a temptation to distrust God and his mercy. Saint Faustina reminds us that when we suffer we are given a wonderful opportunity to rely on God's merciful love. We are called to embrace our cross and follow Jesus, who offered his whole life — particularly his suffering — as a sacrifice to his Father in heaven. We are called to unite our suffering with that of Christ's passion, and seek to foster a deeper trust in the mercy and love of God that sustains us.

////////////

Suffering is the greatest treasure on earth; it purifies the soul. In suffering, we learn who our true friend is.
True love is measured by the thermometer of suffering. Jesus, I thank You for the little daily crosses, for opposition to my endeavors, for the hardships of com-

munal life, for the misinterpretation of my intentions, for humiliations at the hands of others, for the harsh way in which we are treated, for false suspicions, for poor health and loss of strength, for self-denial, for dying to myself, for lack of recognition in everything, for the upsetting of all my plans (Diary 342–343).

//////////

*F*or so much of her life, Faustina suffered the pain and weakness of tuberculosis, experiencing only fleeting moments of good health during her life in the convent. Fevers, chills, constant tiredness, chronic coughing, pain in the chest — Faustina suffered all of this; but she refused to suffer without a purpose. Indeed, she offered up all of her suffering, uniting it with the suffering of Christ in his passion and the pain that he felt when people sinned against him. Faustina trusted in God throughout her suffering, praying that souls would be moved to embrace the Lord's mercy as a result of her sacrifice of suffering:

> O Jesus, how sorry I feel for poor sinners. Jesus, grant them contrition and repentance. Remember Your own sorrowful Passion. I know Your infinite mercy and cannot bear it that a soul that has cost You so much should perish. Jesus, give me the souls of sinners; let Your mercy rest upon them. Take everything

away from me, but give me souls. I want to become a sacrificial host for sinners. Let the shell of my body conceal my offering, for Your Most Sacred Heart is also hidden in a Host, and certainly You are a living sacrifice (Diary 908).

During her later suffering, Faustina was graced by God with the understanding of the interior life of the Holy Trinity. Extraordinary happiness filled her, and she thanked God for enlightening and attending to such a poor creature. As her suffering increased and her day of death approached, Faustina relied more and more on God's grace and mercy. She wrote in her diary: "I don't know how to live without Him. I would rather be with Him in afflictions and suffering than without Him in the greatest heavenly delights" (912).

Suffering in Isolation

Suffering — physical, psychological, spiritual — can be a great isolator. There is a tendency to "close off" from others when we are in pain. The selfishness that oftentimes accompanies suffering can isolate the person suffering from the world around him; it can isolate that person from God as well. A person will focus on himself — his suffering — to the point that he removes himself from the people in his life.

He begins to tend to his own need and abandon loved ones. He can blame God for his ordeal and cease praying.

While self-interest is a necessary element in dealing with pain (a person in pain should seek treatment), suffering does not need to be an isolated and angry period. It can be an opportunity to grow in the love of God and unite oneself with the suffering of Christ.

Suffering is a part of life, a part of every life. The pain of loss, of physical hurt, is unavoidable. It can last for a brief moment or linger for a lifetime. When we suffer, God can seem very far away. It might seem that God has abandoned us, that God could only be present when we are in good health, at peace, and joyful.

When God became man, he sanctified and made holy *every* aspect of the human experience. Every facet of humanity that had once been stained by sin was made holy again now that God had united the human and the divine through the Incarnation. Jesus of Nazareth was born, he lived, he knew joy, felt sorrow, and experienced pain before dying on the cross. Every part of the human experience was made holy by his grace. Even unpleasant experiences such as suffering are opportunities to experience the love of Christ, to share in the suffering he knew, and to offer to take comfort in the reality that God is with us in the midst of our suffering.

Carry Your Cross With Joy

When he walked this earth as a man, Jesus offered everything that he was and all that he did to his heavenly Father. We are called by Jesus to do the same, and this is apparent in the Mass when the life of Jesus and the gifts and prayers of the congregation are offered together to the Father in a sacrifice of love. All that we have to give, we give to the Father in whole. This includes our pain and suffering. This too must be offered to the Father, just as it was offered by Jesus in his own passion and death.

Everything we are comes from God. And everything we do should be done to glorify his name. Jesus said to his disciples: "If any want to become my followers, let them deny themselves and take up their cross and follow me" (Mt 16:24). We are called to follow Jesus Christ as we suffer, and glorify his name in the pain we feel. Why should one separate pain from the rest of his life, when he is called to offer everything he is and everything he does to God? We glorify God's name by our talents, do we not? When we construct something, when we help to raise a child, or when we write a poem we glorify God's name to the best of our ability. This should also be our approach when we suffer. This too we can offer to God in love, because it is a part of *who we are*, and God loves us for who we are, wherever we are, in whatever physical, psychological, or spiritual state we happen to be. He wants us to give everything we have over to him, to trust in his love and mercy. He will provide us the grace to weather any storm.

God gives us the grace we need to weather any storm of pain and suffering. And though we are tempted to focus only on our suffering, to be angry with God for allowing this pain to visit us, and "close off" in a spirit of selfishness from the people in our lives, Saint Faustina reminds us that such temptations come from Satan and must be dismissed:

> November 30, 1937. When I was going upstairs this evening, a strange dislike for everything having to do with God suddenly came over me. At that, I heard Satan who said to me, "Think no more about this work. God is not as merciful as you say He is. Do not pray for sinners, because they will be damned all the same, and by this work of mercy you expose your own self to damnation. Talk no more about this mercy of God with your confessor...." I replied, "I know who you are: the father of lies." I made the sign of the cross, and the angel vanished with great racket and fury (Diary 1405).

The temptation to feel sorry for oneself and question God's mercy in the midst of great suffering can seem overwhelming. The moment this temptation arrives is that point in time when God's grace is needed the most. We must fight the temptation to selfishness, to distrust God, when we suffer. Let us follow the example of Jesus, as Saint Faustina did, and trust wholly in the mercy of the Lord, offering our suffering as a sacrifice to our heavenly Father.

Jesus, do not leave me alone in suffering.
You know, Lord, how weak I am.
I am an abyss of wretchedness,
I am nothingness itself;
so what will be so strange if
You leave me alone and I fall?
I am an infant, Lord,
so I cannot get along by myself.
However, beyond all abandonment I trust,
and in spite of my own feeling I trust,
and I am being completely
transformed into trust —
often in spite of what I feel.
Do not lessen any of my sufferings,
only give me strength to bear them.
Do with me as You please, Lord,
only give me the grace to be able
to love You in every event and circumstance.
Lord, do not lessen my cup of bitterness,
only give me strength that
I may be able to drink it all (Diary 1489).

Let us now pray the Chaplet of Divine Mercy (page 27)....

Reflection Questions

How is my faith life affected by pain and suffering? Have I felt the isolation that can accompany suffering? How have I responded to the temptation to distrust God's mercy, to "close off" from loved ones, in the midst of suffering? What are those crosses in my life that I must embrace and offer to God? Do I make an effort to reach out to those people in my family, in my parish, or in my community who are suffering, perhaps to offer them my services as a practice of mercy and as an extension of God's love?

13
The Desire for Sainthood

Focus Point

////////////

We are all called to be saints. Our Lord wants us to be with him in this life and in the next. He graces us with the desire to be with him, to know the fullness of his love. He provides us the strength and the courage to adhere to his Ten Commandments and live according to his will. Temptation and fear will enter into our lives, but we must be resolute in our trust in God's mercy, always ready to say "yes" to whatever he will ask of us.

////////////

[Jesus said to me:] "Bear in mind that when you come out of this retreat, I shall be dealing with you as with a perfect soul. I want to hold you in My hand as a pliant tool, perfectly adapted to the completion of My works.

"This firm resolution to become a saint is extremely pleasing to Me. I bless your efforts and will give you

opportunities to sanctify yourself. Be watchful that you lose no opportunity that My providence offers you for sanctification. If you do not succeed in taking advantage of an opportunity, do not lose your peace, but humble yourself profoundly before Me and, with great trust, immerse yourself completely in My mercy" (Diary 1359, 1361).

///////////

Nearly eighteen months after leaving Vilnius for her final assignment in Cracow, and less than a year before her death, Sister Faustina made what would be her last eight-day retreat in October of 1937. It was during this retreat that Faustina spoke with Jesus about what it means to be a saint. Through her experience, and coming to a life of complete trust in the Divine Mercy, Faustina realized that every aspect of her faith, including her ability to trust in the Lord, was a result of God's grace.

On the seventh day of the eight-day retreat, Faustina was filled with a tremendous grace — the knowledge that she would become a saint by God's grace — and she overflowed with gratitude:

> I have come to a knowledge of my destiny; that is, an inward certainty that I will attain sanctity. This deep conviction has filled my soul with gratitude to God, and I have given back all the glory to God....

I am coming out of this retreat thoroughly transformed by God's love (Diary 1362, 1363).

Following the retreat, Faustina had gained an even deeper appreciation of God's great mercy, and how that mercy makes it possible for ordinary people to "gather merits for eternal heaven" and become saints (see Diary 1373).

Called to Sainthood

In the Gospel of Matthew, Jesus says to his disciples, "Be perfect ... as your heavenly Father is perfect" (5:48). As modern-day disciples who want to be close to God in our daily lives, we heed this call as well. We follow the Ten Commandments, we participate in the sacraments of the Church, and we practice acts of love in service of God and neighbor. God wants us to be close to him, to work toward the kingdom of heaven on earth, and to meet him in heaven when our time on this earth is finished. He furnishes us with the desire to do so — we are set up for success.

A life of holiness is not set aside only for the priests and religious. There is an all-too-prevalent perception among the laity in the today's Church that the priest is responsible for spiritual matters, ministering to the parish and praying for its members, while the laity has the more practical responsibility of paying bills, raising children, and commuting to work every day. The priest and the laity might meet for Sunday Mass or a parish event, but apart from that the priest is to attend to holiness and the parishioners to their secular lives.

The reality is that we are all — priests and laity alike — called to holiness. Another reality is that holiness can be found in so much of the laity's daily — and seemingly mundane — activities. God is present in all things; it is up to us to recognize him there. When we approach an activity in our lives in a spirit of love and with the intent of glorifying God through that action, we are seeking holiness just as if we were praying inside our parish church.

Think of all the places you go and all the people you meet each day. There are myriad opportunities right there, with those people, for bringing God into the situation, for making a space for holiness. How many times each day do we pass up an opportunity to evangelize? How many times do we fail to recognize a moment where we can teach someone about God's great mercy? We must be aware of the opportunities surrounding us. We need only open our eyes in a spirit of mercy to see the want around us. We will know what to do when we see it.

Do not Fear; Say "Yes" to Love

Any time we open our hearts to God, or make ourselves vulnerable to another, we face fear. There is fear and risk involved in so much that we do. When we are in the midst of change, we face the fear of the unknown. When we come to another person, we face the fear of revealing ourselves to them, and having them know us beyond the previous comfort of a first impression. When we come to God, particularly in the sacrament of penance, we face the fear of voicing our failures to him and giving ourselves over to his mercy. Is it any wonder that one of the most common phrases uttered by Jesus in the gospels is "be not afraid" or "do not fear"? Jesus knows we feel anxious and afraid.

As imposing an obstacle as fear may seem to us, it is nothing in the presence of God. The First Letter of John tells us,

> God is love, and those who abide in love abide in God, and God abides in them. Love has been perfected among us in this: that we may have boldness on the day of judgment, because as he is, so are we in this world. There is no fear in love, but perfect love casts out fear; for fear has to do with punishment, and whoever fears has not reached perfection in love (4:16–18).

Therefore, let us strive to be perfect, to imitate God, and become more like him in love. By this will we overcome our fears. God will grace us along our path, providing us the strength and courage necessary to open our hearts to him and say "yes" to his will. This "yes" we utter is brought about by God's love. His love gives us the courage to do his will and, in turn, open ourselves to others and serve them with acts of love. It is a cycle of love, and it begins with God and carries on in us through our "yes" to his divine will.

Saint Faustina grew in her love of God — and allowed God to love her — to such a degree that temptations and the fear to say "yes" to the divine will became less and less of an obstacle in her endeavor for holiness. At the center of her desire for sainthood was, of course, trust in the mercy of God. As Faustina continued to imitate the love of Christ and pray to him throughout her suffering and into her last year of life, her focus on sainthood became a passionate fire that would only increase. Let us pray with her now:

Most Sweet Jesus, set my love on fire for You
and transform me into Yourself.
Divinize me that my deeds
may be pleasing to You.
May this be accomplished by the power
of the Holy Communion which I receive daily.

Oh, how greatly I desire to be wholly transformed into You, O Lord! (Diary 1289).

Let us now pray the Chaplet of Divine Mercy (page 27)....

Reflection Questions

Do I feel God calling me to sainthood in my life? How am I attempting to incorporate holiness into my daily life, outside of Mass? Do I approach each day as an opportunity to grow closer to God in love? Who are those people that I encounter on a daily basis who might benefit from my humble attempts to model God's love and mercy? What temptations and fears obstruct that path? What practical steps can I make to address those fears? Might I consult a priest, religious, or spiritual director in seeking advice as to what practical steps I might take?

14
Humility in Whole

Focus Point

///////////

God is our Master, and we desire to serve him, offering back to him the gifts he has given us in an attempt to glorify his name. Jesus is our model of perfect human offering to the Father, and we seek to live a life of offering in imitation of his example. At the heart of humility is gratitude, a sense of thankfulness for all good things that come from God, and a recognition that God will care for us always. Our trust in God's mercy is strengthened by our gratitude and by our increasing dependence on God's will over our own.

///////////

O Jesus, eternal God, I thank You for Your countless graces and blessings. Let every beat of my heart be a new hymn of thanksgiving to You, O God. Let every drop of my blood circulate for You, Lord. My soul is one hymn in adoration of Your mercy. I love You, God, for Yourself alone.

My God, although my sufferings are great and protracted, I accept them from Your hands as magnificent gifts. I accept them all, even the ones that other souls have refused to accept. You can come to me with everything, my Jesus; I will refuse You nothing. I ask You for only one thing: give me the strength to endure them and grant that they be meritorious. Here is my whole being; do with me as You please (Diary 1794–1795).

////////////

Christ Is the Perfect Model of Humility

*W*hen God became man in the Incarnation, he did not come to us as an earthly king bedecked in jewels, or as a wealthy member of the higher class, or as a person expecting to be served by the rest of humanity, waited on hand and foot. When God-made-man walked the earth he lived his life as a humble servant, and in the process modeled for our benefit what it means to be truly human. The Letter of Paul to the Philippians says:

> Let the same mind be in you that was in Christ Jesus, who, though he was in the form of God, did not regard equality

with God as something to be exploited,
but emptied himself, taking the form of
a slave, being born in human likeness.
And being found in human form, he
humbled himself and became obedient
to the point of death — even death on a
cross (2:5–8).

If God — who is perfect — lived his human
life as a humble and obedient servant, why
would we choose to live our lives any other
way? We have been shown by God how a happy
and peaceful human person is to live; and he
has given us the desire and grace to do so.

In the same way that Christ lived, Faustina
viewed herself as a servant of Christ and of all
people. As a servant of Christ, she was always
ready to care for anyone in need because she
saw Christ in all people. Faustina wrote in
her diary about an instance in which a young
man dressed in tatters and frozen from the
cold came to the convent in search of food.
Faustina searched the kitchen and found soup
and bread, and she gave it to the hungry visi-
tor. It was then that the man revealed himself
as Jesus and disappeared from her sight (see
Diary 1312). By humbly serving others in a
spirit of love and mercy, as Faustina did in her
Christian life, our own relationship with God
can grow to greater heights.

Faustina's Desire for Humility

In her diary entry of February 4, 1935, Faustina marked a large "X" over the words "From today on, my own will does not exist" (374). Faustina understood very well her status as a human, as a beloved creature of God. As Jesus had taught her, Faustina gave everything over to God. In an act of total submission, Sister Faustina discarded her own will in favor of God's. Of course, this act did not arrive without years of struggle, constant prayer, numerous temptations, and powerful doubt.

Faustina's total submission was tested throughout her life, particularly during the days leading to her death. It was during her final year that she experienced a deep darkness in her soul. Facing strong temptations — temptations so terrible that she would not record them in her diary for fear of scandalizing any person who might read it — Faustina plunged herself into prayer, trusting in God's mercy as she had throughout her life. The Lord advised her:

> First, do not fight against a temptation by yourself, but disclose it to the confessor at once, and then the temptation will lose all its force. Second, during these ordeals do not lose your peace; live in My presence; ask My Mother and the saints for help. Third, have the certitude that I am looking at you and supporting

you. Fourth, do not fear either struggles of the soul or any temptations, because I am supporting you; if only you are willing to fight, know that the victory is always on your side. Fifth, know that by fighting bravely you give Me a great glory and amass merits for yourself. Temptation gives you a chance to show Me your fidelity (Diary 1560).

After hearing these words of mercy and assurance, Faustina understood how the Lord wanted her to face the temptations that assailed her, and she was filled with gratitude.

The Heart of Humility

Everything in our lives — including life itself — is a gift from God. Our family, our friends, joy, laughter, the sacraments — these are all God's gifts. How can we respond to God with anything but gratitude? *Everything* comes from his goodness, from his love and mercy. When we reflect on this for even the briefest of moments, we are humbled into the realization that we owe our very life to God, that we are his servant and he is our Master.

If God has provided humanity with everything it needs to be joyful and at peace, why would humanity ever consider abandoning God for something that is less than the Creator? Why would humanity forsake the Father for something that promises joy and peace but does not deliver, instead leaving its followers empty and anxious? And yet, the people of this world choose those things that are less than God every day. We must always keep in mind the source of all that we have. Gratitude will overflow from our hearts when we keep God in mind, and in our gratitude we will seek to serve the Father as a humble servant, merciful and kind, just as Jesus, the perfect model of humility, lived his life among us.

With Faustina, we pray for a heart filled with gratitude, a humble heart, a heart that seeks to serve the Lord and glorify his name, a heart that is merciful, a heart that trusts in the Lord....

O will of the Omnipotent God,
You are my delight,
You are my joy.
Whatever the hand of my Lord holds out to me
I will accept with gladness,
submission, and love.

Your holy will is my repose;
In it is contained all my sanctity,
And all my eternal salvation,
For doing God's will is the greatest glory.

The will of God — those are his various wishes
Which my soul carries out without reserve,
Because such are His divine desires,
In those moments when God shares
His confidences with me.

Do with me as You will, Lord.
I place no obstacles,
I make no reservations.
For You are my whole delight
and the love of my soul,
And to You, in turn,
I pour out the confidences of my heart.

Let us now pray the Chaplet of Divine Mercy (page 27)....

Reflection Questions

What are some practical steps I might take to deepen my sense of humility? Might I consider reading the gospels on a daily basis and meditating on the words and actions of Jesus, the perfect model of humility? What are those obstacles that hinder me from accepting God's will into my life? As I consider my personality, does pride or a need to control every aspect of my life prevent me from opening up to those opportunities God presents me to deepen my relationship with the Divine Mercy? In an effort to foster a deeper sense of gratitude, might I consider taking a few moments in silent prayer to reflect on all the wonderful gifts with which God has graced me in my life?

15
Fully United With God

Focus Point

///////////////

All throughout her writing and prayers, Faustina asked that every soul give itself to God in full. As the Secretary and Apostle of Divine Mercy, Faustina was given the Image of the Divine Mercy and the Chaplet of Divine Mercy so that the world would come to trust in the mercy of God. In her own life and death, Faustina came to trust totally in the mercy of the Lord, and she embraced death with all the excitement and vigor with which she held her previous life on earth. Faustina's life was a work of love and prayer for souls in need, a well of trust in the divine will, and a testimony to the great mercy of God.

///////////////

When, during adoration, I repeated the prayer, "Holy God" several times, a vivid presence of God suddenly swept over me, and I was caught up in spirit before the majesty of God. I saw how the Angels and the Saints of the Lord give glory to God. The glory of God is so great that I dare not try to describe it, because I would not be able to do so, and souls might think that what I have written is all there is. Saint Paul, I understand now why you did not want to describe heaven, but only said that eye has not seen, nor ear heard, nor has it entered into the heart of man what God has prepared for those who love Him. Yes, that is indeed so (Diary 1604).

////////////

At Prayer to the End

*B*y the summer of 1938, Faustina's condition had steadily worsened to the point where she was too weak to participate in the Mass in its entirety; she was able to receive Holy Communion, however. And though her activities were limited by her health, Faustina made every effort to strengthen her unity with the Father, praying to him constantly for his mercy to enter into the lives of all sinners. Faustina never stopped praying that souls would seek out God's mercy, embrace his love, and repent of their sins.

As she prayed for souls in need of God's mercy, Faustina hoped in her heart that these souls would approach the Divine Mercy in the most beneficial fashion. First of all, she prayed that these souls be entirely open and sincere in their desire for mercy. No secrets should be kept from the Lord, with total trust in the mercy of the Father — regardless of the perceived offensiveness of the sin — serving as the focus of repentance. Secondly, the soul in need of mercy must approach the Lord with deep humility, understanding that as a human being, one is never worthy of — one never earns — God's mercy. God's mercy is all gift, and the soul is the fortunate and poor servant graced to receive such a grace from so high a Master. Finally, the soul in need of mercy must be obedient, fully prepared to move towards perfection by the grace of God. If this soul does not intend to succeed spiritually, it "exposes itself to great misfortunes" (Diary 113).

As her condition weakened and she neared death, Faustina continued further along the path of mercy, seeking God's mercy to greater depths by offering her suffering for the salvation of souls. As Jesus said in the Gospel of Saint Matthew, "Blessed are the merciful, for they will receive mercy" (5:7), Faustina sought mercy through acts of mercy and — specifically during this period of her life — prayers of mercy. She had given everything in her life to God by trusting in his mercy; her impending death, and the increased suffering that accompanied it, provided her one more gift to bring to the altar of mercy.

Complete Unity, Full Reliance on God

The final days of her life provided Faustina the opportunity for prayer and gratitude. She was pleased that her earthly life was coming to a close, and she thanked God for the promise of the eternal life that awaits God's faithful servants. Faustina was also grateful for being able to serve God as a Sister of Our Lady of Mercy, and she expressed this gratitude in a letter to the Mother General. Faustina knew her life was a gift from God, and that the return of her life to the Father was the path of complete trust and reliance on his mercy as modeled by his Son, Jesus Christ.

Saint Faustina Kowalska's life was a progression of total and complete trust in the love and mercy of God. From her days as a child, singing hymns while she worked on her parents' farm, to her teenage years as a cheerful housemaid, to her final hours in prayer, Faustina recognized her sinfulness, acknowledged her place as creature and servant, and relied humbly and totally upon God's mercy. Faustina knew that everlasting life in the Father is never earned. Instead, salvation comes to us all as a gift; we choose whether or not to accept it.

"Trust in the LORD forever, for in the LORD God you have an everlasting rock" (Isa 26:4). These words of the prophet Isaiah express the way in which Faustina lived her life, and they serve as a guide for our own. What else can we rely on, can we trust in, that has the stability and strength of our Lord? Anything in which we place our trust that is less than God will leave us anxious, empty, and without security.

If we trust in the Lord, we can live our lives without fear, without dreading death. It is only the person who has truly lived — and lived in the Lord — who does not fear death. When a person has given everything they are to the Father, they enter into their eternal life without regret, without fear, because everything is in the Father's hands. Trust in mercy, Saint Faustina reminds us, is the heart of a life well-lived.

Following her final confession earlier in the evening, Faustina Kowalska died at 10:45 P.M. on October 5, 1938. A group of sisters from her community prayed beside her bed as Faustina quietly entered eternity in the full glory of the Divine Mercy. With Saint Faustina, we pray....

Hail to You, Eternal Love, my Sweet Jesus,
who have condescended to dwell in my heart!
I salute You, O glorious Godhead
who have deigned to stoop to me,
and out of love for me
have so emptied Yourself as to
assume the insignificant form of bread.
I salute You, Jesus,
never-fading flower of humanity.
You are all there is for my soul.

Your love is purer than a lily,
and Your presence is more pleasing to me
than the fragrance of a hyacinth.
Your friendship is more tender and subtle
than the scent of a rose,
and yet it is stronger than death....
O merciful Jesus, stretched on the cross,
be mindful of the hour of our death.
O most merciful Heart of Jesus,
opened with a lance,
shelter me at the last moment of my life.
O Blood and Water,
which gushed forth from the Heart
of Jesus as a fount of unfathomable mercy
for me at the hour of my death,
O dying Jesus, Hostage of mercy,
avert the Divine wrath
at the hour of my death. Amen.
(Diary 1575, 813).

Let us now pray the Chaplet of Divine Mercy
(page 27)....

Reflection Questions

How has my understanding of God's mercy
developed over these past fifteen days of prayer
and reflection? How has praying the Chaplet of
Divine Mercy on a daily basis affected my spiritual life? How has it affected my relationships
with others? What aspects of Saint Faustina's

personality do I most admire and seek to emu-
late in my own life? What parts of my life
— situations, relationships with specific people,
attitudes toward sickness and suffering — do
I want to focus on giving over to God for the
sake of my growing in trust of his mercy and
humility of heart? Might I consider praying for
the intercession of Saint Faustina Kowalska at
times when I am filled with doubt or afraid to
open my heart to God?

Bibliography

Diary: Divine Mercy in My Soul. Saint Maria Faustina Kowalska. Association of Marian Helpers, 2001.

The Life of Faustina Kowalska: The Authorized Biography. Sister Sophia Michalenko, C.M.G.T. Servant Publications, 1999.

Revelations of Divine Mercy: Daily Readings From the Diary of Blessed Faustina Kowalska. George W. Kosicki. Charis Books, 1996.

Sister Faustina Kowalska: Her Life and Mission. Maria Tarnawska. Association of Marian Helpers, 1990.

Tell My Priests: Words of Our Lord to Priests About His Mercy as Revealed to Sister Faustina Kowalska. George W. Kosicki. Marian Press, 1988.

Also available in the
"15 Days of Prayer" series:

Saint Augustine *(Jaime García)*
978-0-7648-0655-1, paper

Saint Benedict *(André Gozier)*
978-1-56548-304-0, paper

Saint Bernadette of Lourdes *(Francois Vayne)*
978-1-56548-311-8, paper

Dietrich Bonhoeffer *(Matthiew Arnold)*
978-1-56548-311-8, paper

Don Bosco *(Robert Schiele)*
978-0764-807121, paper

Saint Catherine of Siena *(Chantal van der
    Plancke and Andrè Knockaert)*
978-156548-310-1, paper

Pierre Teilhard de Chardin *(André Dupleix)*
978-0764-804908, paper

The Curé of Ars *(Pierre Blanc)*
978-0764-807138, paper

Saint Dominic *(Alain Quilici)*
978-0764-807169, paper

Eugene de Mazenod *(Bernard Dullier)*
978-1-56548-320-0, paper

Charles de Foucauld *(Michael Lafon)*
978-0764-804892, paper

Saint Francis of Assisi *(Thadée Matura, O.F.M.)*
978-1-56548-315-6, paper

Saint Francis de Sales *(Claude Morel)*
978-0764-805752, paper

Henri Nouwen *(Robert Waldron)*
978-1-56548-324-8, paper

Saint Jean Jugan *(Michel Lafon)*
978-1-56548-329-3, paper

Saint Katharine Drexel *(Leo Luke Marcello)*
978-0764-809231, paper

Saint Louis de Montfort *(Veronica Pinardon)*
978-0764-807152, paper

Saint Martín de Porres: A Saint of the Americas *(Brian J. Pierce)*
978-0764-812163, paper

Meister Eckhart *(André Gozier)*
978-0764-806520, paper

Thomas Merton *(André Gozier)*
978-1-56548-330-9, paper

Brother Roger of Taizé *(Sabine Laplane)*
978-1-56548-349-1, paper

Saint Elizabeth Ann Seton *(Betty Ann McNeil)*
978-0764-808418, paper

Johannes Tauler *(André Pinet)*
978-0764-806537, paper

Saint Teresa of Ávila *(Jean Abiven)*
978-0764-805738, paper

Saint Thomas Aquinas *(André Pinet)*
978-0764-806568, paper

Saint Vincent de Paul *(Jean-Pierre Renouard)*
978-1-56548-357-6